LEAP IN

LEAP IN

A Woman, Some Waves, and the Will to Swim

ALEXANDRA HEMINSLEY

PEGASUS BOOKS
NEW YORK LONDON

Leap In

Pegasus Books Ltd
148 West 37th Street, 13th Floor
New York, NY 10018

ISBN: 978-1-68177-433-6

10 9 8 7 6 5 4 3 2 1

Printed in the United States of America
Distributed by W. W. Norton & Company, Inc.

For Lottie, the greatest
sister of them all

PART I

CHAPTER ONE
From the Shore

I thought I could swim, I really did.

It may have been because I could run. It may have been because I wanted to swim. It may have been because I only ever did ten minutes of breaststroke at a time, or splashed and bobbed off a warm beach or in the pool at the gym.

But I really couldn't swim.

I used to watch them, The Swimmers. I used to see them to my left when I got in the pool to do my three or four lengths after a session at the gym doing weights or trying to use the running machine. Or, even better, I'd see them in the sea when I was running along the beach. There was something other-worldly about them, as if by not actually being *on* the earth but being *in* it they had become somehow more than human.

The pool swimmers always had a specific brisk walk as they came from the changing rooms. It just oozed 'I'm not here to fuck about'. Their goggles would usually be on already, making eye contact with them impossible. Their gift, their glamour, lay somehow behind their rubber and plastic eyes, shielded like a superhero's. Then they'd just slip in and . . . start. The transition from poolside human to slick, slippery silverfish took seconds. Their faces vanished beneath the surface, their arms pulled the water ahead of them away as their front crawl effortlessly propelled them forward. It was beyond me. Where was the bit where they emerged, panting and ruddy-faced, needing to break into breaststroke after three quarters of a length? Or hung around at the end of one of the lanes and stared into the middle distance, catching their breath and rolling their eyes at the unholy effort of it all?

They never did. They'd just get in and get going. I would console myself with what I told myself was my strong breaststroke kick and glide along, the water dividing my face at my nose, leaving me looking and longing, a covetous hippo. My eyes swivelled and my heart yearned.

The sea swimmers were another species altogether. I would only know them by the steady rotation of their arms and perhaps the neon of a swimming cap. Often they swam so far out that I could not tell if they were in a wetsuit or a regular swimming costume. They would slide through the sea, ageless, genderless, a part of the water, a part of the view. It seemed rigorous, but also peaceful.

As the skyline bobbed up and down in my vision, bouncing with the gait of my run, the sea swimmers seemed to exist in a world somehow less aggressive than the one I ran in. I knew the ache of ankles, knees and hips after hitting pavement or tarmac for hours on end, and I had grown to love it – I associated it with warm baths after battles won, with the meditative state that running gave me and with the huge emotional lessons it had taught me. Within five years I had gone from someone for whom any sort of exercise was theoretical – a nice idea, but something for others, for the 'sporty types' – to someone who had run five marathons. Running had been my entry point into a world where I understood both my body and the elasticity of my limitations so much better. It improved my confidence, it improved my relationships, and it improved my body. But now I had grown a little impatient with the burgeoning running industry, with its endless heavily marketed events, its relentless reliance on technology that cost you a week's salary to tell you that you weren't quite as good as last week, and above all its obsession with time and distance.

I began to wonder about the freedom, the less jarring tiredness, and the sense of well-being that swimming out there in the deep might give me. It looks wonderful, I'd think, but it can't be that easy to become part of the ocean.

It had always been there, the ocean. As a child, I'd stayed with my grandparents in Cornwall, or my mother's family in Trinidad and Tobago. During the turbulent years of my twenties in London, when there was no ocean, I would console myself with long walks along the Thames, or the Regent's Canal or around the ponds in Hampstead. Then, on moving to Brighton, the sea became a daily fixture in my world.

I ran in Brighton. I ran in Hove. There was rarely a run that wasn't at least partly spent watching the ocean melt into the sky at the earth's curve. There were fast, angry 5K runs, done at a furious pace after a bad day at my desk. There were slow, anguished 10Ks, run straight into relentless winds coming directly off the Atlantic. And there were long, hot marathon runs, drenched in sweat and longing for the solace of seawater. Once, three years ago, I worried I was getting sunstroke and headed off the path and straight into the sea to cool off. But only as far as my hips.

Even when I left the city and went night-running high on the South Downs, from the very tops of the hills I could still see the blackness of the sea. Without realising it, whenever I ran, I tried to run near water. I ran along the Hudson in New York, shrieking at the other side of the Atlantic during a rainstorm, exhilarated by the churning water as much as the bridges that seemed to be strutting from island to island. And I ran the bay in San Francisco, parallel to the sailing boats and the swimmers, one eye on Alcatraz's moody shadow and the Pacific beyond. Whatever else I saw, wherever else I ran, however else I felt, the sea seemed to be alongside me, reassuring in the constancy of its presence.

At home, it felt so much part of my experience that for a couple of years I neglected to realise that in all these years of watching the sea, being guided by its definite shoreline, pacified by its glacial calmness and lifted by its twinkling surface, I had never swum in its shimmering waters. Exactly the thing that had entertained me as a runner made me rigid with terror as a swimmer: up close, you never quite knew what you were going to get.

When I finally grasped that looking at the sea a lot was not exactly the same as swimming in it, I felt its urgent pull. I longed to feel surrounded by the salt water, to let it carry me along, to become part of it. I would stare at the horizon, dreaming, then take a huge breath of salty air and let my gaze drift from the swimmers to a boat turning or a dog barking, and think, But when do swimmers breathe? And with that question, the swimming dream would be over.

I had lived in Brighton for nearly five years when I finally got into the sea. It was the morning of my wedding. A morning that, quite frankly, I had never thought would come. During those long marathon training runs, the early starts and the wind-beaten miles, I had made peace with the fact that perhaps marriage wasn't for me. Through running I felt my body grow stronger and my self-reliance more robust. I actively forged the me I wanted to be, and I felt a weight lift as I grasped how much of my future was entirely down to myself alone. I didn't have to keep internet dating if I didn't like it. I didn't have to keep going to parties just in case I met someone. I didn't have to keep scouring my contacts for an old colleague with whom there was some unresolved sexual tension. I could let it all go and concentrate on running, my friends and my family. So I did, as relieved to have found my place in the world as I was to realise I didn't have to keep waiting for someone to join me.

Of course, with that realisation, it was only a matter of months before D, one of my favourite people on earth, a long-nursed and barely admitted crush, appeared on my doorstep, armed with the sort of declaration of love I had previously thought belonged firmly on the other side of my Netflix screen.

It was as if a door had opened and there was an entirely new room in my heart. One apparently infinite and filled with potential. I was in love, and I realised that my interpretation of what that meant had always been wrong. It was no more restrictive than it was the answer to all my problems. Quite simply, I had found the person I had spent several years comparing all potential boyfriends to, and he was all mine.

Two years later, on the morning of our wedding, I did something else I had never dreamed I would: I finally made it into the sea.

The week that we got married, the sun came out. We had all just about given up hope, and then suddenly, the day that the umbrella to match my wedding shoes arrived, so did the summer. The night before the ceremony, I went out for dinner with my family and we walked back along the seafront to the B&B where they were staying, each of us lapping on an ice cream despite it being after dark. Over calzone and slightly too much red wine, I had joked with my brother that I should start my wedding day with a sea swim. Our sister, days from giving birth to her second son, goaded us, telling us to do it for her, then giggling at the ludicrousness of the plan. We laughed back. Of course it wouldn't happen!

I had forgotten all about it by the time I got home and saw my wedding dress hanging on the back of my bedroom door. Eight hours later, I woke up feverish with anticipation, unable to fathom how I might possibly spend the seven hours until it was time to walk down the aisle. No one was even supposed to arrive at our flat for another three hours. I texted my brother on the off-chance, and half an hour later he turned up in his swimming trunks, with his phone and his goggles in his hand.

Within five minutes we had crossed the busy seafront road and were standing on the shore. Me, my brother and my fiancé. My dad, a little bewildered by the non-running turn of events, had turned up too – on the strict condition that he had to be back before his hotel stopped serving breakfast.

The sea was smooth, calm and full like a bath. There were none of the feathery white peaks that alternately frightened and delighted me on breezier days. The sun was still struggling to ease its way through a gauzy layer of cloud, lending the view an Instagram-esque filter, and slightly muffling the noise along the beach. The water didn't glisten; there was barely a horizon. An opaque greeny grey simply met a slightly glossy blue as the earth curved away from us. There was a boat far out where the two colours met, but it was early, so apart from that we had the sea to ourselves.

My future husband and I stood on the beach holding hands while the others faffed with electronics and towels. It didn't seem real, this idea that we might just go for a swim as the mist rose from the water and the sun burned through the cloud higher in the sky. It was a morning I'd never imagined I'd have; I was about to do a thing I had never believed I would do; I was a me I had never dreamed I would get to be. He squeezed my hand and nodded at the water.

'We can't stand by and watch, can we?' he said.

'Sometimes you just have to leap in,' I answered, stripping off quickly and darting for the water, dragging him by the hand.

My brother giggled. My dad fiddled with his camera, not wanting any part of the madness but not wanting to miss a moment of it either.

We ran at the final few inches of shore, the pebbles of Brighton's beach pinching and prodding the soles of our feet like a vengeful reflexologist. There was a second's relief as we hit the water and the shelf of pebbles gave way to the sea. Another second and the temperature hit us like electricity. How did it do that? How could a ring of cold around your ribs hit you behind your eyes? We yelped, we splashed each other, we gasped as it reached our lungs, our hearts. I could hardly breathe, and I didn't know if it was the excitement, the cold or the terror.

Then, suddenly, we were in. We were swimming. The water

was all around us and that electric charge had subsided. In its place was a coolness, a sense of invigoration, as if someone was somehow tweaking the focus on the day, making it sharper and more real. We seemed to be the only ones in the sea, and the sound of our breathing was all I could hear, apart from the odd muffled seagull that seemed cranky about an early start.

We swam out, a cautious breaststroke, aware that we knew nothing of what the tides were doing or where we might be pulled, despite the apparent stillness of the water.

'We're in! We're in! My first time in the sea after living here for nearly five years!' I whispered.

'Whaaaat? How could you not have done this before?' asked my brother.

And with that, he was gone, swimming front crawl into the distance. I glanced around and saw that D was doing the same. Both of them carefully but steadily looping their hands over their heads and pulling the water back beneath and behind them. I swam further out, then turned to look back at the shore.

I thought I knew the seafront inside out. I'd seen it in rain, storms, glorious sunshine and at 4 a.m after ill-advised nights out and gut-wrenching arguments. But I'd only ever seen it from dry land. From the sea, it was as if my home town was in tilt shift. Where once I'd pounded the pavements in January, entirely alone, now I saw a hundred little figures, each making tiny movements of their own. There was our home, one small flat slotted into the buttercream Regency facade of the terrace we lived in. From the land it was huge and solid, but now it looked like a toy, a mere accessory for a doll's game or the sort of thing you'd lay alongside a model railway.

As I turned slightly, I saw the seafront square where I'd lived years before, and the front door at which D had appeared that happy summer before he even held the title 'boyfriend'. I looked along the water and saw that he had waited for me a little way ahead, so we swam together a while parallel to the beach. We saw the bar where our wedding party would later be held, still shuttered against the elements. We lay on our backs, holding hands, supported by the salt water, and watched the seagulls overhead as we stared into for ever.

Where a runner sees the world in close-up, with time to view each passing tree's leaves as they fall, each yellow road marking as it fades through the seasons, each dog truffling treats from the roadside, I realised that a swimmer sees the long shot. A ball thrown across a beach, a seagull swooping for an unwatched doughnut half a mile away, a rumbling lorry meandering by as if being pushed by a four-year-old.

There was a coolness, a stillness to these moments as we felt the water lapping us and watched our city from afar. My breaths were still deep from the effort, and my skin tingled from the salt and the chill. The sun began to break through the clouds, and after about half an hour, we realised we should be heading home. I stepped out of the water and gazed back at the scene laid out before me. I was glad it was today that I had made the leap. I had held my heart back for long enough. I now felt a visceral urge to seize everything life was throwing at me and live more intensely than I ever had.

Days later, as my new husband and I sat in a Parisian bar, two glasses of pastis on the small circular table between us, we discussed that magical swim. It had felt so exactly the perfect thing to do at that precise moment. As we chatted with the confidence of the just-married, we decided we would keep it up.

'We should become regular swimmers!' I declared with the sort of elaborate hand gesture that four days on the Continent and just as many glasses of liquor can encourage. I could see it so clearly; we'd be that magical couple who swam in the sea every day. As the pastis fug thickened, I felt delighted with myself that our swimming plan was decided, and casually mentioned working on my front crawl with the same confidence with which I'd discussed how we'd never fall out over Christmas plans, never look at our phones in the bedroom and always chat about literature over dinner. I was going to be *so good* at being married.

Days passed in a haze of museums, oysters and nauseating hand-holding in endless cafés. We kissed on the Eurostar home, and I told the bored taxi driver that we were on our way back from our honeymoon, trying to eke out every last minute of the magic. When we got home, we knew exactly how we wanted to begin post-honeymoon life: heading for the sea. Our suitcases were left unpacked, the salty butter and the bottle of Pernod we'd purchased that morning hastily chucked in the fridge, and we scampered to the beach to feel the water as soon as possible.

But this time it was colder than before. Yes, the sky was blue over Brighton, but over us, in the sea, there were low, dark clouds gathering. We laughed with shock at how different, how much more hostile, it felt. Neither of us really wanted to admit that this wasn't the homecoming we'd hoped for, so we stayed in the water trying to work out if the clouds were heading in or out. Wind whipped up out of nowhere, blowing my hair across my face.

'It's so much colder than last week!' I yelped, determined not to be the one to admit that the honeymoon glow might be fading.

'I know – it's made my wedding ring look enormous,' replied my husband, holding out his hand to show me how loose it was on his shrunken finger.

With that, a huge wave hit him from behind and, almost in slow motion, the ring flew off into the sea.

For a few seconds we just stared at each other, not quite able to take in the fact that less than a week since he had put it on, his wedding ring was almost certainly lost for ever. Suddenly the bad weather didn't seem like the worst thing to have happened since our return.

'Oh my God,' he mouthed at me.

'What do we do?' I replied frantically. 'Where can it be? Everything's moving . . .'

'Stay there. I'll run home and get my goggles,' he said.

'Okay, I won't move. I'll try and find it with my feet.'

D ran up the beach towards our flat. I saw him head behind the iron railings to our front door, wrapped in only a towel. The minute he slipped out of sight, the wind whipped up even higher, causing the sea to froth around me and surge below. I tried to stay in the same place, but swells kept knocking my legs out from beneath me. I tried to grasp with my toes, searching in the sand for anything that could be a ring . Again and again I would find a lump, convinced I had it, then lift my foot to my hand under the water only to see that it was a small shell, or a bottle top. Never a ring.

A couple of minutes later, the sky was almost entirely dark, a dirty layer of cloud lying low above me. The sea was similarly dark – no green or blue was left, only swirling sand and churning opaque water, throwing me from side to side more violently with every passing moment.

I pushed wet, salty strands of hair back from my face and spat out the water I was swallowing as it splashed into my face, its grit catching between my teeth. I could just about see D leaving the flat, closing the gate behind him. This time he was a blur, and even as he neared the water's edge I couldn't hear what he was saying over the noise of the rain hitting the waves. He ran back in towards me and grabbed me.

'You've moved so far along,' he said. 'We'll never find it.'

I was no longer anywhere near parallel to the front door. The water had pushed and pulled me. Its strength, what it was capable of without me even realising, sent terror trickling down the small of my back.

'Quick, dive,' I gasped. Even as I said it, I knew I didn't really want him to. I wanted him above the water where I could see him, hold him. But he ducked down, desperately grasping, searching for anything that caught the light as a band of gold might. Again and again he submerged, returning again and again with shells curled in endlessly frustrating curves, or just fistfuls of hardened sand. Eventually I threw my arms around his neck and begged him to stop. The tide was coming up the beach fast, and the water that had been chest height was now up by our necks. I was shivering, my teeth chattering. The sea had turned, the ring was gone. The dream was over.

Between sobs, I told him it didn't matter, that the ring clearly hadn't fitted properly, that it wasn't meant to be. Eventually we surrendered it to the sea and staggered home, cold to the bone and silent. The ring was lost for good, and my confidence in the water seemed to have been dragged out with it.

Two days later, we returned to the jeweller's to buy a replacement ring. A bell tinkled as we pushed the shop door open, and we stood in the entrance holding hands like sheepish schoolchildren. The staff who had helped us a couple of months ago all looked up in synch, then down to our hands, before stealing quick glances at each other.

'Was it the sea?' one of them asked.

'Or a river?' said another.

'Here, or on the honeymoon?'

A single tear started to roll down my cheek.

'How did you know?' I asked.

'It happens a lot more than you think,' said the kind woman who had helped us choose our original rings. 'But it doesn't make it any less upsetting.'

We nodded feverishly, D's shoulders relaxing as he realised he wasn't the first, and was unlikely to be the last, to lose a brand-new wedding ring. Before long he had been refitted for a second, slightly smaller ring, and the episode was behind us.

Except it wasn't. Because I was still angry with the sea. I knew it was ridiculous; the solemn metal detectorists and their regular dawn patrols made sure I was reminded almost daily that we weren't the only ones to have lost something precious to the deep. And I knew we could have lost a lot more.

I was also hurt, and scared. I had never felt the rage of an ocean turning against me before, and that half-hour had left me more frightened than I had been in years. To feel the water swell and churn beneath me, to see something as solid as gold simply vanish with what felt like a vindictive sleight of hand, had left me with a knot of anxiety I had no idea how to unpick.

In all honesty, seeing our flat flooded a week later was not the best cure. We went to bed happy after a lovely weekend, and were woken at 3 a.m. the following Monday by a huge thunderstorm playing out in the skies above us. Sleepily I snuggled up to my husband, who mumbled something about how crazy it sounded out there. For nearly an hour we lay in a silent embrace, unable to fall fully asleep while the storm raged on. After a while, I became convinced that there was a strange, echoey chill to the bedroom. I could hear what sounded like a single drop of water dripping. But there were no taps in the room; none were even within earshot. Eventually curiosity got the better of me and I swung my legs around to get out of bed and investigate. As I did so, both my feet hit several inches of water.

At first I was horribly confused. Where had it come from? There was no leak, no drip from above, yet the entire room was filled with water, at least ankle deep. My husband sat bolt upright at the splash, splash, splash of me crossing the room to the door, then leapt out of bed himself when he heard me scream from the living room. It wasn't just the room that was filled with water, but the entire flat.

As the electrical storm grew ever more violent, the thunder cracking what seemed like inches from us, the water continued to rise. I pulled on a pair of leggings and a T-shirt and ran outside to call the emergency services.

On the street, a fleet of fire engines raced past the front door. The lightning was hitting the sea with a viciousness I had never even imagined, let alone witnessed. Several people were out in the road, looking in despair at the water filling their homes too. I tried to call again and again, only to be cut off by the severity of the weather or the busyness of the number I needed. Eventually I begged the emergency services to come and help us, screaming with terror as further claps of thunder from directly above rattled the pavement I was standing on.

'We can't come,' they told me, as I strained to hear against the wind, the sirens, the thunder. 'If you are able-bodied and can get out of the property, we have to go elsewhere first . . . We have to prioritise the elderly and the sick . . . The whole seafront is flooded . . . We will get to you when we can.'

I listened helplessly, awash with fear and exhaustion. For the second time in a week, wind and water whipped my hair across my face, stinging my eyes, the strands catching in my mouth.

Once I was sure that the fire service had all our details, I resigned myself to returning to the flat and trying to save whatever we could from the deluge. We discovered that the water had crept in silently underneath the door to the back yard, flooding the flat in minutes, leaving the carpets sodden, ruining hundreds of books, turning years' worth of accounts to illegible mush, wiping treasured photographs of their images and destroying countless electricals. But we still had each other.

After hours spent bailing the water out, we stood in the kitchen with a takeaway coffee, trying to laugh at the situation with friends who had come over to help. As I sat on the countertop – the only dry seat in the house – I saw a copy of a book I had ordered while in Paris, ready for our return: *Swim*

Smooth. It was a large, almost magazine-sized paperback, and it was so wet that I was able to take an end in each hand and squeeze it so that a full mug's worth of water oozed out in a thick, noisy trickle.

Our wedding was only a couple of weeks ago, but already everything I had ever felt about the sea had changed. I'd ordered that book in the spirit of optimism, seeing the sea as a wonderful ally I was about to get to know better. Now it was the enemy. Thief of rings, wrecker of homes, menace to married life. I hated it.

I had become more afraid of the sea than I knew it was possible to be. Where once I had longed to relive the sense of freedom it had given me as a child, now I wondered if I'd ever go in it again. On top of that, I was furious with it for its unpredictable moods, its slippery menace, and with myself for not being strong enough to fight it.

Later that week, as we sat in a local takeaway, part of our daily routine now that we were rendered semi-homeless by the flood, I tried to articulate my rage to my husband. He understood how sad I was that he had lost his wedding ring, but seemed a little perplexed by my taking it so personally.

'It's like it hates me!' I muttered into the laminated menu. 'Why does it want to ruin the start of our marriage? It's supposed to be the happiest summertime of our life and I feel like I've spent most of it rotating my paperbacks around the terrace to dry them quicker.'

'It doesn't care,' he replied sadly. 'You can't pick a fight with an entire element.'

I stared at the illustrations of noodles and bit my lip. Maybe he thought I couldn't pick a fight with an element, but I was damned if I was going to let myself be beaten. I had tasted the terror of not being able to swim properly and I didn't like it. I knew from past experience that we choose the selves we want to be.

The grit was in the oyster now. It was the sea versus me, and I would throw everything at this fight, so determined was I not to be deemed the loser.

CHAPTER TWO

Summer

Within the month, I had booked us on to a one-day open-water swimming course.

D was keen to be supportive – we'd been married only a few weeks, after all. But I could tell from his special face of gentle and considerate listening that when he saw me, he now saw a powder keg needing to be handled with the utmost delicacy and diplomacy for fear of damaging explosions. Woe betide the being who dared to suggest I couldn't accomplish something I had set my mind to. He had long ago learned this, most notably when he texted me as I was halfway round a horribly hilly half-marathon, suggesting that I didn't have to finish if I didn't feel up to it. When he saw me later from the crowd and waved in support, I flicked a V at him and called him a wanker for not believing in me.

'Of course I'll come too,' he said. 'It will be fun.' I didn't miss his slightly pale smile. It was a look not dissimilar to the one my sister would give me when I suggested we swapped clothes. He is a glasses wearer, and has an uncanny habit of being able to tilt his head to the perfect degree, blocking proper eye contact and rendering him inscrutable.

Earlier in the week, I had called the organisers of the course, which was based at the Brighton Swimming School, keen to know whether it would be okay that I wasn't great at front crawl. I reassured them that I was fit, and a strong breaststroke swimmer, and they told me that as long as I could do ten or twenty lengths, I would be fine. The description of the course on the website sounded so perfect – a morning in the pool refining technique, lunch over a talk about the tides, then an afternoon in the sea under careful supervision. It all seemed so innocent, so manageable.

It wasn't that I *knew* I couldn't do ten or twenty lengths of front crawl. It was more that I had never really tried. I knew I could do a few strokes; I definitely remembered doing that in swimming pools at gyms or on holidays over the years. I had just never tried to do it consistently, for any length of time, or with any sort of regulated breathing. What I needed, I told myself, was some focus, a few pointers, a bit of motivation. After a full day of tips and hints I would surely be on my way to a life of sea swimming!

Yes, I was sure of it. And D, staring stoically out of the window as I repeated my thoughts to him the evening before, almost certainly agreed with me.

The course began at 8.30 a.m. on the other side of Brighton, but we had to be there even earlier, as we were due to hire wetsuits for the open-water part of the day.

It was a gorgeous morning. The sky was entirely clear and the air was warm even as we left the house just before eight. As we waited fifteen minutes for a bus, slowly marinating in our own sweat, D remarked on how lucky we were with the weather. I think he might have mentioned it again as I grumpily hustled us into a taxi, now clammy with the stress of it all and really quite bored of the delights of a warm day.

The heat was the sort that, unless you're merely stepping from an air-conditioned car to an air-conditioned building, seems to warm you from the inside out. The sun was still too low for it to be piercing; instead, I simply felt as if I'd been lightly microwaved for perhaps thirty seconds. Too warm, tacky to the touch, with thighs that felt bigger than they ought to as they nestled against each other on the faux-leather taxi seat. By the time we made it to the pool, there were beads of sweat all along my hairline, and those at the nape of my neck were now trickling down towards my back.

The Brighton Swimming School pool is pretty much the most boring pool I have ever seen. It doesn't have the deluxe hum of a spa, or even a fancy gym. No huge plastic bucket of fun toys for children, no water chutes, nor even a steam room. It's just a pool, albeit one that is clean and solid. It is where the beach lifeguards are trained, where triathletes ready themselves for competitions, and where children and adults alike are taught to swim. But it is not a place for recreational splashing. It is a pool that means business.

Within minutes of arriving, we were directed to the room where we could choose from the selection of wetsuits for hire. There was a rack of pre-loved suits, each one dangling at a jaunty angle from a wire coat hanger like a discarded snakeskin. D, tall, slim and broad-shouldered, does not challenge the conventional wetsuit silhouette and was off to the changing room within minutes. My body, however, proved more demanding.

Since I'm not especially tall, my figure initially seemed suited to a medium wetsuit. One was held against me.

'That looks about right,' said the assistant.

I removed the towel I'd placed around my neck to mop up my nerve sweats and showed the assistant my boobs. And then my bum.

'But the fabric . . . will it get round all this?' I asked anxiously. If you held the wetsuit against me front on, the shape very much matched mine, but side on – well, there was little hope.

A long glance up and down. There seemed to be some sort of maths going on. A distant memory of being taught to read Ordnance Survey maps where the lines ran closer and closer together floated across my mind.

'I think I should take a large,' I said, preferring to pre-empt the inevitable verdict.

'The thing is, wetsuits are supposed to feel really tight. It's how they work,' explained the assistant. 'So if you put this one on and it feels a bit loose, just let me know and you can swap it for the medium.'

I headed to the changing room. For what transpired to be the loneliest ten minutes of my life.

I thought I had known true loneliness. There had been so many Saturday evenings spent with only Danish crime dramas and a bar of Lindt 'Touch of Sea Salt' for company. Countless weddings where I was the 'fun' one at the table, only to dart home alone and melancholy lest someone expect me to cop off with an usher. And school reunions where everyone compared childbirth stories while I provided a jolly tale about falling over during a marathon training run by way of comparison.

But none of those things were true loneliness. Because the loneliest place on earth is halfway into, halfway out of a wetsuit. And that is where I got stuck.

My body was by now clammy all over, radiating heat as a result of the balmy day, the warmth of the pool environment and the rush of blood created by the prospect of getting changed. I dived right in, plunging my calves into the lower half of the wetsuit, then tried to yank the rest up from the waist. I say waist, but the neoprene was very, very far from there. All I had managed to do was create a baguette-width roll of wetsuit just beneath my hips; an unwelcome arse-shelf. The spongy flesh that made up my haunches was now sitting in a magnificent display of rococo arse-cleavage above the neoprene corsetry. The part of my legs within the wetsuit seemed to have gone cold, possibly as a result of inadequate circulation, while the skin directly above the haunches was becoming ever stickier with sweat, proving an effective braking system for any fabric I tried to pull over it. Where had all of this *me* come from?

I unravelled the waterproof baguette, letting loose an enormous squeak as the coated exterior of the neoprene popped apart and the arms flailed out from the bulk of the suit. I yanked and yanked until the top half fell forward. I needed to put my arms into the sleeves, but the gusset of the suit was still hanging between my legs at mid-thigh. I yanked at the fabric, trying to pull it up my thighs, desperate to grab a proper fistful of material but trying not to jab into the slick coating with my fingernails. Repeatedly I had to twist my hand to the side and pinch as much as I could between my thumb and the lower edge of my forefinger. Slowly, slowly the suit legs inched their way up my actual legs. With a flourish of frustration, I yanked the body up my torso. As soon as I had done it, I realised my mistake: on account of the crotch still being a few inches too low, the neckline was now sitting across my boobs, dividing them into four, the sleeves dangling from my armpits.

Sweating, exhausted and increasingly paranoid about the ever-more-likely chance of someone else entering the ladies changing room, I was desperate to sit down. But the logistics I was now dealing with had rendered this absolutely out of the question. The only way out was forwards, so I took a deep breath, wriggled my hands down and forward into the low-hanging sleeves and hoped for the best.

I should have known that it would be at this moment, when I was fully immobilised, that the door would swing open. I heard the clunk of a bag on a bench before I turned myself around to smile limply at my fellow swimmer.

'Hello,' I said. 'I think I'm stuck.' I lifted a hand in greeting, painfully aware that it was still encased in rubber. I had yet to get to the ends of the sleeves, and without the use of my hands to yank the fabric, I had just spent ninety seconds reliant on shoulder-shrugging alone to shuffle the wetsuit back over my clavicle and shoulders. Behind me, my arse was still hanging out of the bottom of the zipper.

'Do you need . . . some help?' the woman asked. I could tell that she was trying to be polite and encouraging. But I was past that.

'Yes please,' I said, biting my lip so as not to let my voice break, and submitting meekly as she hoicked the shoulders back, pulled the two pieces of fabric together and forced the zip up.

It felt as if I were wearing an iron maiden rather than a wetsuit. My heart was hammering, I was breathing using only the top fifteen per cent of my lungs, and the rubber around my neck seemed to be forcing itself into my throat. I waddled out of the changing room to the corridor, where I called for my husband.

'They told me to say if it was too loose,' I said. 'But it isn't, is it?'

'No, it's not,' he said. He offered nothing else, aware that any further words were unwise.

'Thank you,' I replied, and returned to the changing room to take it off for the morning's pool swimming. As I undid the zip and breathed out, a whoosh of freedom rushed over me. My shoulders dropped, my heart slowed a little and I let myself breathe in using my stomach. I hung the wetsuit next to my sports bag and consoled myself that I didn't need to think about it for a few hours.

By the time I got to the pool's edge, most of the rest of the course participants were already doing their warm-up. About six men and a couple of women were ploughing up and down the lanes with a sense of purpose I was not sure I could even fake. Patrick, the instructor running the day, asked me what sort of level I was, and I replied that I needed to be in the slowest lane.

'No problem,' he said cheerfully. 'That's the left-hand one. We're just doing a ten- to twenty-length warm-up to get loosened up and so I can have a look at everyone's technique.'

'Okay,' I said with a smile, shoving my hair into the swimming hat I'd been handed on arrival. A pause. 'Does it matter if I don't do it all front crawl?'

'Just do what you can manage. We're here to improve,' said Patrick with a smile.

I edged my way to the left of the pool and walked down the steps into the water, shaking with trepidation. D saw me as he turned at the end of his lane, and gave me a quick thumbs-up. I felt my face turn crimson as I dunked my head underwater, ready to swim. How had I not understood that ten lengths was merely the warm-up, not the sum of the swimming we'd be doing on the day? I waited until the only other person in my lane was at the opposite end of the pool, then started to swim.

I had no idea what I was doing. But I gave it my all.

Determined to propel myself forward from behind with strength and vigour, I kicked as hard as I could with my legs, windmilling my arms to finish off the look. I made sure to keep my elbows locked as I swooped my arms up and out of the water, my hands slapping down ahead of me seconds later. At first I managed to do eight strokes before flicking my head up, straight ahead, and gasping for air. The next time, I managed six, then five. Finally I had made it to the other end. But at what a cost.

My chest was starting to seize up, constricted as if there were a metal brace around my ribs, my legs were flooding with lactic acid and my heart was drumming a beat I was sure could be heard in the water around me. I started the return length with a little breaststroke, keeping my head above the water in the hope of catching Patrick's attention.

'So, um, was this the sort of thing you were after?' I asked. Patrick was walking up and down the side of the pool, watching us. I desperately hoped he would answer me, because that way we could carry on a conversation and I could pretend that that was the reason I wasn't returning to front crawl.

'Sure, just keep going,' he said non-committally. 'Whatever you can manage . . .'

Dammit.

I took a huge gulp of air, pushed my face back into the pool and stared down at the bottom. I could feel my heartbeat quickening as I thrust my chest deeper and held on to the air I had taken in, eking it out slowly, as little at a time as I could manage. I did another six or so strokes before I turned my head, almost rolling over, exhaled the remaining air I'd been holding onto and took another huge inhale.

Once I reached the end of the pool, I decided to use D as my next decoy ploy. I leant over the lane barrier to see how he was doing, but he took no time at all to tell me he was fine, so there I was, still somewhat out of breath, and only two lengths down. I had to head back up to the other end.

This time I figured it would be easier if I just did the swimming in as few blocks as possible, only stopping for the utter faff of breathing every now and again. I lifted my head out of the water – I had made it to the deep end in record time! Now, to head back. I managed three strokes before having to stop and fall into breaststroke again. This time, it wasn't just my lungs that were starting to burn. My fingers and toes had begun that grim fizzing that I had long associated with my first few ill-fated runs.

Learning to run had taught me all about that horrible feeling as your limbs, lacking oxygen while having to work harder than they're used to, start to squawk for help as you gasp for air. I know so many women who have experienced it, and have kept running as fast as they can for fear of not looking like a runner. Then, after three minutes, they return home, swearing off running forever. After all, how can it be good for you if it makes the roots of your hair, your fingernails, your internal organs hurt?

'Just keep a steady pace,' I have told so many disheartened runners. 'It does hurt those first few times, but it's just the unoxygenated blood doing its best to help limbs flailing with the unfamiliar. Try not to go too fast, and have a little patience. Get your breathing at an even pace, and in about ten minutes things will settle down. *Just give it ten minutes.*'

TEN MINUTES.

What the unholy hell was I thinking, telling people to hang in there for 'just' ten minutes? How had I thought this was helpful? I couldn't keep going in the water for even five more minutes! I only had seconds left in me, without repeatedly resorting to breaststroke with my head up. My runner's legs were no help in the pool, only serving to weigh my body down. And those words of advice that I had been dispensing in good faith to great results now seemed like a hollow taunt.

After about five lengths of hell, Patrick stopped me and pointed out that while the issues with my stroke could be dealt with at a later date, what I really needed to sort out was my breathing. He told me to try and breathe every third stroke; something I discovered later in the day was called bilateral breathing, because if you're breathing every third stroke, you're breathing on alternate sides. I nodded and did my best, but it still felt like some sort of impossible party trick.

It seemed there wasn't enough time to get everything I needed to do done. My legs were powering like a steam engine, my arms were still looping around with elbows locked, and in the time it took me to do three strokes, I was not even close to having let go all the air I was taking in. I explained this to Patrick.

'You have to force the air out,' he said. 'At the moment you are trying to swim with a huge bag of air inside of you.' He held his palms up, fingers splayed, against the back of the lifeguard who was standing on the side of the pool. 'Think about how huge your lungs are. And think of them filled with air. That is what you're effectively dragging along with you. It's like you're trying to swim with a huge plastic bag tied to your foot.'

I understood his point, I really did. But putting it into practice seemed impossible. As did his final piece of advice: 'Relax.'

Once the torment of the warm-up was over, we spent time doing various exercises to practise skills such as sighting, and turning around a buoy, as well as a demonstration of why bilateral breathing is so vastly preferable if you're going to be in open water. In these short bursts of swimming, when we were taking it in turns to just head for a buoy eight metres away and then do a turn around it, I was fine – there were huge gaps of time while the others had their go when I could stand around watching, chatting, trying to calm myself down.

After a few hours of this, we were out of the pool and heading to a meeting room for lunch and talk of tides, sea conditions and parasympathetic breathing.

Over a feast of salads and pasta, we talked about what we hoped to get out of the course. I was surprised to hear how many of the burly-looking blokes had been happily swimming in pools for years but felt they needed some help to get them over the psychological barrier that swimming in the sea presented. I seemed to have approached things back to front, having gambolled into the ocean a month ago, head full of memories of childhood holiday fearlessness, only to have the confidence whipped away from me as fast as my husband's ring had been.

'It's so irrational! I was fine before!' I said, whilst shovelling lunch into my mouth as fast as I possibly could.

'What's worth remembering about open-water swimming is that there are no irrational fears,' said Patrick. I frowned. This didn't sound like great news. 'After all, you can never entirely know what's beneath you at any given time when you're in the ocean. You can have a pretty good idea, and you can be careful with where you swim, and what the tides are up to. But you can't ever know for sure. There is just . . . too much ocean, and too little human.'

I stared at my plate. He had a point. If it was the case that the house always wins, then perhaps this battle to beat the sea was ill-conceived.

After lunch, it was time to go into the sea. This time I was prepared for getting into a wetsuit; like the rest of the team, I went for a 'legs only' approach until we had walked down to the east beach, between Brighton's much-loved 1880s Palace Pier and its perhaps less-beloved 1980s Marina. Patrick was swimming with us, and there were other instructors there too – one in a kayak and one on a paddle board. They all had radios enabling them to talk to each other, and they had set out buoys demarcating our swimming zone.

Before being allowed to enter the sea, we were all reminded of the acclimatisation exercise that we had discussed and practised in the pool that morning. The technique involves moving slowing into the water before submerging face, then ears, then back of neck, then taking five deep breaths, each time fully exhaling to push all the air from the lungs. The idea was to get in and get the body accustomed to the temperature while letting water seep through the wetsuit and keeping your breath at a steady pace.

We've all seen YouTube videos of pranksters leaping into icy lakes then reappearing, gasping and yelping as if there is an electric shock beneath the surface, and they're hilarious. But that stinging feeling is less amusing when you're surrounded by unfamiliar churning water and you're already nervous about having to swim through it. The aim of acclimatisation is to avoid this state of panic as well as keeping things physiologically steady.

The reality was a little different. I walked straight in, having had my wetsuit zipped up by my husband, and immediately drew a sharp breath that made my lungs feel as though they too had just been zipped up from behind, leaving only a matchbox-sized space at the top. It was as hard to exhale as it was to inhale, my body instinctively clinging on to that pocket of air it had snatched as the cold had hit me. It was by now early afternoon on a blissful summer's day, so I had planned on the temperature being quite bearable. But the difference between the water and my body, warm after twenty minutes chatting in the sun, was immense.

I looked around me to see the others making those first tentative dips of their faces into the water's surface. I tried it too, but found the cold so startling that I couldn't keep my face in for long enough to exhale even half the breath I had taken. I took another gasp and tried another dip, this time just scrunching up my eyes and attempting to hold still long enough for the water to creep round the sides of my face and into my ears. Before long, my entire head seemed to be chilled from within. I lifted my face and let out a huge exhale, remembering too late that I was supposed to have done that while my head was still under. I tried a couple more times, but before long the team was heading for the swim zone by the buoys. It was time to say goodbye to the reassuring pebbles beneath my feet.

As we paddled further out, the sea started to get choppier. The sunshine meant that it was a busy Saturday on the seafront, with boats going to and from the marina and jet skis clamouring round the pier like water-bound starlings. The movement they were creating in the water was passed towards the shore, and seemed to be hitting us again and again.

We were told that first of all we would be trying a simple triangular swim around the three buoys – a total distance of perhaps two hundred metres. The rest of the group, better acclimatised to the water than I seemed to be, headed off in a pack with no hesitation, creating a world of kicked-up, foaming water behind them. Even D vanished on command, lost in the throng.

They seemed to hit an immediate rhythm, moving together almost like ducklings. I could see that they were using the drafting technique we'd been taught only a few hours ago – following in the wake of faster swimmers to take advantage of already parted moving water. But they were all faster than me, and now too far ahead for me to feel the benefit of that wake. Even if I had had the necessary speed to catch up, I'm not sure I would have tried, as I was worried about being kicked in the face or swum over. I had heard horror stories of triathletes receiving black eyes and smacked jaws, or even having their heads unceremoniously shoved deep into the water so that a bigger swimmer could pass over them, and now those thoughts were flooding my mind. I stayed where I was, treading water by the first buoy, panic rising in me as what felt like the metal girder of my wetsuit seemed to circle my chest ever tighter.

'It's a meditative act,' they had told us. 'Gentle, repetitive movements with controlled breathing. Isolated from the world and your troubles, you're in your own bubble – literally!'

This is not meditation, I thought, as another wave slammed mercilessly into my face, forcing me to swallow frothing seawater just to keep an airway free. It's barely survival.

'The wonderful thing about the water is that it fully supports you – none of that impact you get with running!' I remembered them saying.

But the water isn't supporting me, I thought as it whipped my exhausted legs from side to side while I tried to kick against the waves. It's beating me up.

'There's nothing like the sense of harmony you get from swimming in the sea,' they had declared. 'And it's so refreshing! A total high!'

I am not refreshed, I thought as I craned my neck to search for the buoy I was aiming towards, the harsh salt stinging my eyes until they were useless while sandpapering my nose and throat. I am in harmony with nothing and no one.

I flipped myself onto my back and sobbed.

I tried several times to get going, but even when one of the instructors paddled alongside me in a kayak so I felt safe, even when I started way behind the others to avoid their churned-up water, even when I tried breathing on just the left, or just the right, or counting four strokes instead of three, I still couldn't make it from one buoy to the next without stopping, breathless and thrashing. I couldn't find a space for myself in the water. When I turned to breathe, a wave would come. When I tried to kick, I would feel the swell move stronger than me. When I aimed for calm, flashes of potential danger would flood my mind.

After a time, the panic turned to rage again. The hard-won friendship I had finally forged with my body over the preceding few years seemed to be crumbling around me.

Where once I had been convinced that any sort of sporting activity was not for me, running had taught me otherwise. I missed those dark mornings when I had run alone, learning to love my limbs as the strength emerged from them like sturdy thighs appearing from a sculptor's marble. But today, today felt as if none of those mornings had ever happened. The sun's glare highlighted the excesses of my flesh within the wetsuit. The waves' power increased the lack of mine. My husband's encouraging smiles were just a foil for the sense of dismay with myself that I was experiencing all over again. How could this truce with my body, the one I had worked so hard and so long for, now be falling apart?

I was a fit person! I had listened to all the lessons! I had the right attitude! It seemed ridiculous that this same woman who joyfully told others that they could conquer whatever challenge they chose, who had not even been afraid of the ocean a month ago, who cheerfully assumed that this would not be a big deal, was now reduced to this limp, flailing wreck. But I was. And in the water, you don't get the chance to stop, to walk, to take a moment on the pavement.

I clung to the safety of treading water with my head up, feeling suffocated by my neuroses as much as my wetsuit, and spent the remainder of the afternoon in the company of Kim, the lifeguard paddling the kayak. She assured me that I had everything it took to be a sea swimmer, and that I just had to work at it.

'I can tell you're a swimmer,' she reassured me. 'You just need to relax.'

Oh, how I wanted to believe her.

I eventually crawled back onto the pebbles, furious, indignant and exhausted. But I knew I would be back. Because I had an inkling. An inkling that this was the beginning of my next big adventure. Slowly, as the day had progressed, I had realised the truth of what becoming a swimmer would entail. It wasn't just about me accepting myself any more. That was only the start of it; I also had to learn to accept the water.

CHAPTER THREE

Autumn

The evening of that one-day course, I collapsed with an exhaustion of a type I was entirely unfamiliar with. I was sleepy like I hadn't been since childhood. After years of training for marathons, I had come to accept the aches of repeated impact on tarmac or trail. My muscles would feel tired and my feet would feel sore. The post-training buzz was accompanied by a buzzing in my joints that I recognised as miles clocked and progress made. But this . . . this was altogether different. There was no negative physical impact from the exercise I had done – no sore knees, no aching thighs, and no blisters from sodden socks. After over four hours in the water, I felt utterly drained, but utterly pain-free. My rage at myself and the ocean had subsided somewhat, leaving me with a strange sort of peaceful exhaustion, more akin to a post-massage sense of relaxation. If this was as bad as swimming got, maybe it was worth persevering, I thought, before falling asleep and forgetting all about that momentary glimmer of positivity.

Throughout the rest of the summer I kept an eye on the water, waiting until the weather was perfect and then running into the sea to try again. I would manage four or five strokes before panicking and flipping onto my back to let myself breathe at the sky, floating and hoping. I headed to my local pool in time for the early-morning slot, with the aim of working out a better technique, alone and unembarrassed by the presence of other swimmers. Instead, I discovered that the crack of dawn was when the most confident swimmers arrived, powering through the water unencumbered by ditherers like me.

I confided the truth about my disastrous efforts to my brother when he came to stay for the weekend, and he in turn confided that he had not enjoyed swimming until he had taken a handful of lessons to improve his stroke and discover a breathing technique he was comfortable with. I begged him to impart his wisdom, so he told me to lie face down along the back of my sofa while he manipulated my arms and legs like a marionette, trying to show me what a decent swimming stroke was. I was grateful, but the next time I got into the pool it became clear that I really wasn't any the wiser.

Eventually, a fact I had been trying desperately to ignore was becoming unavoidable: I needed help. I was going to have to go back to swimming lessons. The prospect was appalling, reminiscent of pitiful early teen years, when the traumas of unexpected periods, shameful verruca socks and changing into swimming costumes loomed large. Taking on any sort of formal learning as an adult seemed distinctly unappealing. As a fourteen-year-old taking a life-saving course and diving for black bricks in a pair of old pyjamas, I had been sure that by my late thirties I would have been shot of such indignities. How did I *still* not know everything I needed to in order to live the life I wanted? It felt like weakness to require the help of teachers all over again. I was married now; I didn't need classmates any more.

But as the summer marched on and married life settled into a routine, a sneaking suspicion crept up on me: perhaps more learning, a fresh project, in a new environment, was just what I needed. Until a month before our wedding, D had worked in London, with early starts that required him to live there for most of the week. Within weeks of our return from Paris, he had a new, significantly better job a ten-minute commute from the flat. Home went from a domain almost entirely ruled by me and my needs – from the hours I worked to the times I slept or the food I ate – to one that seemed to suddenly involve an awful lot of new-found compromise. Despite considering ourselves the very definition of a modern couple – I hadn't even worn a white dress at our wedding! – we now found ourselves managing the same readjustments as 1950s newlyweds who had only spent snatched moments together prior to marriage. In short, I had someone under my feet so much more than I had ever been used to. Some time with my head in water, entirely alone and unable to chat with anyone, suddenly seemed like bliss.

Thus, swimming lessons were handsomely rebranded. If I weren't borderline allergic to the term and all its connotations, I would have referred to it as 'me time'. Instead, I chose to see it as a strength to ask for help, and committed to taking a nine-month course organised by the same Pool to Pier swimming school that had run the one-day course we had both attended. Starting in September, it promised to teach the basics of front crawl in a context working towards open-water swimming, before moving classes to the sea in early summer and finishing with a swim between the two piers in Brighton – the main Palace Pier and the now derelict West Pier. A fresh mission to undertake in the first year of marriage!

This time, however, I was without the support network I had had in the past. There were no reassuringly dark pavements to run along during quiet evenings, no kindly paternal advice, no reassuring knowledge that simply doing the training would make everything else easier. When I began running, I'd had my dad's wealth of marathon advice to lean on. This time, there was no one in my life with the kind of experience I could have done with. This time, I had to surrender to the fact that I did not know how to do something and that I wanted to learn. And I was going to do it in a swimsuit, in front of a group of strangers.

Until recently, I had never been particularly self-conscious about being in a swimming costume. I never swam in pools unless on holiday, and only owned flattering bikinis made for sunbathing rather than doing laps. Swimwear was fun wear. There were no worries about seams that might shift if I exerted myself, or what a rubbing lining might mean for my stroke or my ability to breathe: if I were wearing swimwear, I was relaxed, warm and predisposed to have a good time. If anything, it reminded me of the freedom of childhood; bright, colourful clothing to be frolicked in. To splash and be splashed in. To create happy memories in.

As the years went by, the glee associated with wearing as little as possible was replaced by new, less appealing emotions. The first few moments of any holiday became more uncomfortable – the revelation of white flesh that first morning at the pool, an unfamiliar expanse of thigh after months of UK drizzle in opaque tights; a sensation of being emotionally vulnerable as well as almost physically naked.

And this new situation was taking these anxieties up a notch. The summer was over, the pool had horribly unflattering strip lighting, and I was there to learn. I was already in a position of vulnerability, having admitted that I simply couldn't swim properly. I was expected to concentrate and try hard, not relax and mess about.

As I stepped from the changing room, my white thighs under the greenish lighting looked flaccid and soft to the touch, like an old peeled onion. My feet, dry from a summer in sandals, with the final millimetres of a neon pedicure clinging to the tips of the nails, resembled the onion skin itself.

From the changing room to where the instructors were gathering was not even the length of the pool, but the walk seemed endless; a distance I'd rather not cover while this, well, uncovered. No one batted an eyelid as I emerged, but it didn't stop me from imagining saloon doors swinging closed behind me, and a Sergio Morricone refrain from whistling through my mind. Standing there, exposed and alone, I felt like the new cowboy in town, facing a bar full of hardy locals.

At one end of the pool were some wooden balance benches of the sort I had only ever seen before in school gymnasiums. I sat down, immediately locking my knees together lest, as I suspected, my bikini line were less than perfect. Sitting on a slab of wood one foot off the ground did not create the same silhouette that reclining on a sunlounger usually did. I appeared to be 85 per cent thigh, 10 per cent sweat, and a pair of swimming goggles. My stomach folded, leaving three rolls of flesh stacked neatly on top of each other, like the pale, curved loaves of French bread in my local bakery. I longed for the halcyon days when I felt self-conscious in running wear. How had *that* ever bothered me? It came down to my ankles! It allowed for two layers of fabric across my belly! And it did not betray visible sweat marks until I took it off.

I admonished myself for feeling embarrassed. I'd just spent a year of my life telling women to forget what they looked like when they exercised and focus instead on what they could see.

Think of the positives! I would tell them. No one is looking at you!

I tried to tell myself the same.

But as I did so, an endless carousel of swimsuit images floated across my mind. Each time I had looked at swimwear online, it had been modelled on toned, athletic twenty-two-year-old bodies. When I bought a bikini in store, the merchandising displayed Amazonian goddesses with skin as smooth and reliable as injection-moulded plastic. Every time I had looked into swimming pool membership, the promotional material had boasted youthful, glistening flesh stretched over rippling muscles. As with running gear, it was impossible not to be sold the promise of an ideal when you were so far from it. Those doing the selling seemed oblivious to the fact that when they told us, 'This could be you!' we could actually hear them adding, 'But it's not!'

The endless use of these images, as well as the pernicious, corrosive and sly term 'bikini body' are phenomena that I would happily see wiped from the face of humanity. Sure, I get that that phrase refers to you being your best for your two weeks in the sun each year, but the damage done by the implication that we are substandard for the remaining fifty weeks is so much greater than any fun and sunshine could repair. It doesn't matter that most women only need to think about wearing swimwear for a fortnight per year – the language around it works on us daily as it drip drip drips on our souls like the salt water hitting Brighton's beautiful wrought-iron seafront. Eventually we are worn down. We begin to believe that a bikini body isn't one that is simply us, wearing a bikini, by the water, relaxed and enjoying ourselves. We begin to believe that it is an unattainable goal, available only to those who buy the right supplements, trainers and cosmetics. We begin to believe that it is a body whose secret is shared discreetly among magazine editors and Instagram superstars only. We begin to believe that it is a body that belongs to other people. It is not *this* shameful body, here, always here, beneath our clothes; the body whose shape we have to reveal if we want to experience the glorious freedom of running around a park on a spring day; the body whose flesh we have to expose if we want to feel the gleeful weightlessness of floating in the sea as the sun hits the water like sequins.

The enormous, unnavigable wall of advertising images and 'helpful' diet suggestions from wellness gurus and health magazines does little to dispel this ubiquitous decree that we should all be a little more similar, a little more manageable, if we want to enjoy our own bodies. Because these bodies actually are our own – they do not belong to the advertising executive who chooses a model pretending to run rather than an actual runner for shoe advertisements. They do not belong to the surfwear designer who will only use six-foot blondes to showcase their product. They do not belong to the men who stare as we drop our towels and walk towards the water's edge, trembling as much at what others are thinking as at what might befall us once we leap in. These bodies are ours, and we must use them as best we can.

I sat on my bench, anxiously wondering what the others on the course might look like, how they might compare to me, and whether I had signed up for something hopelessly inappropriate for my abilities. How was it possible to feel so large and yet so small at the same time? I felt as if I were about to walk the plank rather than take a recreational swimming lesson.

The bodies that emerged from the changing room were nothing like the ones I was used to seeing selling me swimming costumes. There were shoulders wider and stronger than mine, but legs visibly weaker. There were flatter bellies, and flabbier buttocks. There were slimmer calves, smaller hips and neater toes. But there was softness, endless softness, and a variety of flesh: different colours, different textures and different degrees of muscle tone. It was as if the endless parade of orangey plastic skin that accompanied all images of swimwear and swimming was made up of fake display fruit compared to the marvels of the ripe market stall that I was now seeing.

These, my classmates, were largely women of around my age but there were some a decade younger and maybe a couple older. We all looked utterly different and yet the same. I had stepped out from beyond the mythical wall of bikini bodies. Now, I walked among humans. The relief!

We were introduced to each other by Kim, Julia and Patrick, who had taught me in the summer. They gave us each a Pool to Pier swimming hat, which immediately rendered all introductions largely useless, as without their hair I could no longer recognise anyone. (I still find it nearly impossible, and have spent hours of my life swimming with people whose names I am still not quite sure of. Facebook profile pictures rarely help.) We were divided into lanes according to ability: those who had taken the course the previous year and were using it as extra training; those who were already okay swimmers but who wanted to prepare themselves for open water; and those, like me, who could not do a single length of proper front crawl.

My classmates in the other lanes needed little instruction and busied themselves almost immediately with swimming, but four of us were told we'd be focusing on the business of deconstructing front crawl, re-understanding it and then learning it entirely from scratch. Determined not to play for time with 'intelligent' questions while fighting to catch my breath, I tried my utmost to clear my mind and simply do whatever was asked.

Nevertheless, I *had* been hoping for something a little more dynamic, something that felt more like actual swimming. For our first exercise, we were simply asked to practise breathing out. First above the water, then, pulling our knees up and exhaling deeply, letting ourselves sink to the bottom of the pool's shallow end. The aim was to demonstrate how bodies are easier to submerge when they're less full of air, and by the third time I felt my bum bounce off the tiles a few feet below me, I was convinced. Despite having been told it only a few weeks earlier, I now understood that our lungs were really little more than two huge sacks full of air.

Next up, we were asked to combine our new-found exhaling skills with some movement. Specifically, pushing off from the end of the pool, first with our breath held, then while giving a large exhale. The difference in the distance we could cover was extraordinary: you simply don't get very far if your lungs are clinging desperately to air, puffing you up like a beach ball. The third time, we were asked to push off both exhaling *and* extending our arms in front of us with thumbs side by side. As we whooshed forward, I understood how much faster the water was able to move around me if I created a more pointed, dynamic shape.

This act of emptying our lungs in motion while reaching forward also made it easier to push our heads and chests into the water, creating what I was told was a crucial sensation of almost swimming downhill. This apparently kept our legs up, parallel to the water's surface, in an ideal swimming position.

This was not an instruction I had ever received before regarding my body's position in the water. At some point in the last thirty-odd years, I had most definitely missed a meeting. Somewhere in the dustier recesses of my memory, I remembered being clearly told (not long after dunking my feet in a disgusting tray of Dettol) that front-crawl swimmers should not create too much splash with their feet. In fact, I had long understood that the very best swimmers were the ones who left barely a ripple. In order to remain nice and calm when I swam, I had always made a conscious effort to keep my feet a good ten to twenty centimetres below the water. Now the breaking news seemed to be that our bodies should really lie as flat as possible on the surface, if anything with chest and shoulders slightly lower than the rest. Apparently it was perfectly possible to have your feet in this position and not create a world of splashing. I was unconvinced.

The volume of new information I was going to have to take

on board – and the effort it was going to take to relearn so much muscle memory – began to dawn on me. Putting even this small new skill into practice seemed more than a little challenging. During July's one-day course, I had relied almost entirely on my legs. Convinced that after years of running they were my only source of strength, I had tried to power up and down the pool propelled by the force of my kick alone. Now it was slowly being revealed that trying to push my body ahead from behind was never going to be as efficient as learning to pull it elegantly forward, using my legs as mere stabilisers. In not knowing what I was meant to be doing with my arms, I had effectively been trying to shove a panicking octopus up and down a pool in front of a dense metal pole.

This was bad news. Not only were my legs my hard-earned pride and joy, they were also heavy with muscle. I had an arse built by squats, and thighs used to carrying me on four-hour runs. Dense with fibrous muscle and padded generously with the curves I'd inherited from my Latin ancestors, they were less than easy to keep high in the water – particularly given my ongoing misgivings about holding my face down, as a result of my breathing still being so erratic. Frankly, my legs were never going to make an effortless and dignified transition to back-seat passengers.

And as the lesson progressed, just how much of my front-crawl stroke I had been doing incorrectly started to become clear. As well as attempting to push myself from behind instead of pulling from in front, and keeping my legs and feet low, I had tried to lock my elbows so that my arms were entirely straight for as much of my windmilling rotations as I could manage. I had also been lifting my head up to breathe instead of tipping it sideways. The list was endless, and it was becoming apparent why I had found those few strokes I had managed so utterly exhausting: I was doing almost everything in the most difficult way possible, and on top of that, I had been trying to do it in a state of panic, with largely unoxygenated blood coursing through my system.

What was needed was for me to learn an almost completely new portfolio of muscle memory. Arms needed not to swing up and round with elbows locked, but to leave the water elbow first, high and neat. Hands needed not to meet ahead of me, barely an inch apart, but should be wide, allowing me space to get a good swing down through the water. That swing needed not to fade out limply below me, but to turn into a push back until my thumbs were almost grazing my thighs. Legs needed not to kick fiercely from the knee but to move softly, flowing from the hip, while feeling floppy and loose. My head needed to turn tightly, chin almost to shoulder, so I could find air to breathe in the tiny pocket my own head had created as it moved through the water. Oh, and I needed to develop a strong enough core to keep me rocking gently but controlled.

The more we talked about what a good stroke was supposed to look like, the more I realised that what I had based my own Frankenstein's monster of a style on was a messy amalgam of swimsuit advertisements, music videos and Instagram posts. I had never really stopped to study what someone moving fast in the water in front of me was doing – largely because of pool etiquette, but also because I had fallen for the same trick that I had with running: I had believed what the most dynamic, glossy-looking images presented to me had suggested. With running, it was a series of promotional pictures – daft photographs of six-foot models flying through the air in jewel tones and hi-tech fabric, often landing aggressively heel first, their faces a picture of total serenity. Trying to copy this was about as practical as it would have been attempting to give birth based on what I had seen on a soap opera.

Unpicking my problems – both mental and physical – seemed a ridiculous undertaking that first week. But the instructors assured me it was doable in time. Julia herself, a beacon of calm on the side of the pool, told me that she had started as a student on this very course only a few years ago before going on to become an instructor. It became clear that in order to break the cycle of the old, incorrect and inefficient muscle memories that I had randomly stored, I needed to take on a series of tiny, broken-up pieces of information, introduced to my body (and mind!) slowly, week after week. Unlike running, where I headed out one day and didn't look back until I hit a wall of injury, this time I was going to have to destroy and rebuild from the very beginning.

It was a long autumn. As the summer of our wedding turned slowly into a bleak, rainy and windswept winter, once a week, whatever else was happening, I turned up for my swimming class. Almost without fail I would arrive consumed by a sense of dread, convinced that this would be the week I finally admitted defeat. I would dither whenever I could, playing for time, clinging to the side of the pool to catch my breath and sip my water. But I always left the pool convinced that I was improving. And it wasn't just the stroke that started to feel important. It was the feel of the water, the way it held me where it never used to, the slippery sensation of being nearly naked despite the onwards march of winter, the curious roar of underwater as I let my head plunge in length after length, regardless of my misgivings.

The variety of drills we did now seemed infinite, but week in, week out, the basic structure of the lesson remained the same. We started with a ten-length warm-up (much of which I swam breaststroke for several weeks), followed by a series of exercises that took front crawl entirely apart then slowly put it together again until what had felt utterly alien became something closer to automatic.

In those first few days of learning to run, it had been all about fitness: in order to run further, or faster, I just had to keep doing it, consistently, and the results began to reveal themselves. With swimming, fitness was secondary to the art of making things easier for myself: by developing a better front-crawl stroke (or indeed one at all), I was nurturing the skill of needing less effort as I swam. This time, fitness could come later.

For the first few weeks, most of the lessons focused on what we were supposed to be doing with our arms. The process of staying alive during this almost vertical learning curve was helped enormously by the use of fins. Like the sort of flippers worn on holiday for snorkelling, but shorter and stubbier, they helped my legs stay up and my body to keep moving forward, so that I could undertake the various arm drills without exhausting myself too much to either concentrate or even continue.

We would swim on our sides, fins on, to get used to the tilt of our bodies in the water; we would pull our arms up along our bodies as if a zip between thumb and side was being undone from thigh to mid ribcage; we would swim holding a plastic pole in front of us to keep our hands spread apart instead of tipping inwards towards each other. We would roll our shoulders forward, one then the other; we would practise breaking the surface with our hands tipped at a slight angle, before stretching even further in front of us under the water, as if reaching for something at the back of a high shelf; we would practise just shoving our hands back along our sides to our hips to make our stroke as long as possible.

I could usually manage these drills, thriving on using new parts of my body, finally surrendering to the fact that learning as an adult was not admitting a weakness but developing a strength. I loved the curious sensation of having my feet in fins, almost divorced from the process of the muscles in my arms, which were growing and learning with every passing week. And once I was strong enough, I loved the help provided by the mysterious float I suppose I had always seen by poolsides but had never really noticed before: the pull buoy. Designed to be wedged between the top of the thighs, giving your legs and bum balance and stability in the water, it slowed my stroke down enough that I was able to swim without fins, while also harnessing my ongoing instinct to kick as hard as I possibly could, endlessly exhausting myself.

As I had suspected, my legs were my nemesis. Every time I lifted my head to breathe, my thighs would start to sink and drag me down. Despite getting my arms moving as they should, I was struggling to put them together into any sort of cohesive movement with the rest of my body. I reminded myself of my new baby nephew, so often caught with one leg wedged beneath him as he struggled to use his core to push himself forward into a crawling motion. He could see he needed to reach, he could feel the strength in his legs, but he just couldn't quite make that tip into a single, seamless movement rippling from head to toe.

I was learning to love the water, I was learning to trust my arms, and my new muscles were growing – helped now by consciously working on them in the gym to develop stronger shoulders. But I just wasn't learning to breathe. Again I reminded myself of my baby nephew. Too young to talk, he would nod and smile when we said words at him, but no matter how he shaped his mouth, he was too small to copy us and speak himself. I too was able to listen and nod as I heard how important it was to get my breathing right, but, unable to make my body follow suit, I felt paralysed for much of the lesson: specifically the bits when the fins or floats were taken away and we were asked to swim normally.

As I stood in the shower after a particularly frustrating session, I remembered the conversation I'd had with D the evening of that one-day course. We had been discussing my panic and fury during that day, and I'd tried to understand why even though he wasn't an especially great swimmer, he had been left unruffled by plunging his head into the water and getting going.

'Once I'd got the exhaling, it seemed to click into place,' he simply stated.

The exhaling. It struck me that this was at the root of my problems. It wasn't the breathing, but the exhaling. I could breathe in; I was desperate to, even if I hadn't finished breathing out. But here was the problem: the exhaling. Memories of yoga classes, meditation apps and even the simple act of trying to calm myself down before exams, meetings or dates floated through my mind. I thought of running, or having run. Being crouched over on the side of the track, gulping for air, after sprinting practice three years previously.

A deep inhale was instinct. But I was going to have to learn to exhale.

CHAPTER FOUR
Learning to Exhale

Within days of this revelation, thoughts and memories of breathing out consumed me. Whenever I had a moment alone, I would try and think about my exhaling, how it felt, what I was doing and how it connected to what else I was doing. Before this, the most time I had ever spent thinking about breathing was during my ill-fated yoga phase. I'd turned up, week after week, longing for limbs like a pretzel and my own personal slice of calm. I enjoyed the breathing, and was in no doubt that it helped me concentrate and achieve more than I would have been able to otherwise. But in the end I had given up, exhausted not by the exercises, but by the urban hustle of being in rooms packed to the rafters in order to increase revenue, endlessly emailed about loyalty cards and new products, and fed a slow, vague drip of nebulous philosophy about inner peace and miraculous recovery from injury. In short, the vibe of corporate millennial yoga meant my lip now curled at most talk of exhalation.

Yet I thought about it all day, every day. And all night, every night. I had to learn to do it if I wanted to be able to swim.

Biomechanically, our heads are the heaviest part of our bodies. At the moment, every time I took a breath in water, I needed to lift my head up, high and long enough to finish exhaling and *then* to inhale, wasting energy that could have been spent on gliding through the water.

So I would sit, on the train, in cafés or waiting for meetings in corporate lobbies, thinking about my breathing. I'd move my head around, to remind myself how heavy it was – no wonder I was finding it a faff to lift it out of the water long enough to get everything done. On the bus one day I became so entranced by my own breathing that the lady next to me asked if I was okay, or if I was about to pass out. While running, I took to leaving my music at home so I could listen to my breath alone, and learned how much faster I could run while keeping each inhale and exhale steady with the pum-pum, pum-pum, pum-pum of my shoes hitting the tarmac.

While flicking through old photographs with my sister, I saw one of myself when I was still a smoker. I was with a group of friends in a pub, back in the days when smoking inside was perfectly normal. My eyes were smiling at the camera, but my face was turned away and up, exhaling smoke from the cigarette in my hand. I could remember the evening perfectly: a shared birthday party for my sister and me in a pub in an upstairs room in Notting Hill. It was during the brief period that we lived together, both of us single, both of us carefree, both of us smokers. Those few years now seem like madness – today, even walking past someone smoking on the street makes me queasy.

But looking at that image that seemed both so alien and so immediately me, I realised that there was one thing I had always loved about smoking: the exhaling. The moment of quiet when you silently pulled the cellophane wrapping from around a new packet, tapped the end of a cigarette on the box, lit it, and then, after hearing the fizz of the tobacco burning with the inhale . . . the exhale. The purse of the lips, the sag of the shoulders, the release of the smoke.

When I first moved to Brighton, I had started smoking again for a brief few months. My small flat, from which I could see a corner of the sea, was accessed via a little garden. I would sometimes go and sit out there, particularly during the lonely summer that I moved to the seaside. I'd had my heart broken within weeks of arriving in the city: my new boyfriend turned out to already have a girlfriend, confusingly also called Alex, and was attempting the almost admirable feat of juggling two identically named, very similar-looking girlfriends, in two different cities.

The evening of the day the other Alex emailed me to let me know of her existence (hot tip, adulterers: if you own a house, and therefore a bank account, with someone, don't expect them not to wonder why you're frequently withdrawing cash in Brighton all of a sudden), I sat on the stone steps in that little garden, listening to the seagulls above, and opened a fresh packet of cigarettes. I had spent most of the afternoon piecing together a fabric of timelines and lies, slowly realising just how many of the decisions I had made over the last few months had been based on empty promises. As I lit the cigarette, my hand was still shaking, adrenaline pulsing to my very fingertips. The first exhale, and my shoulders slumped. That's it, no going back, I thought. I couldn't move back to London, and I would never see that man again.

As my eyes rested on that twelve-year-old photograph, and I remembered that now historic heartache, I saw my relationship with cigarettes for what it had really been. It never was – it never is – about a passion for inhaling toxins. It was about tiny moments carved out of a life pulsating with chaos and uncertainty, a chance to go and quietly let out a deep exhale. A socially acceptable, and understandable, cool-looking exhale. At bus stops when I was fretting that my bus would never arrive, outside pubs when the throb of the music over heightened chat or quicksilver flirtation was getting too much, and on those cool stone steps as I felt my heart softly implode. Each drag, on each cigarette, an exhale: a release.

It was no coincidence that within weeks of starting training for my second marathon, I gave up smoking again – this time for good. I have not had a cigarette even touch my lips since the night of my birthday party over seven years ago. A party where, I now realise, I spent most of the evening outside smoking, as an excuse to talk to the good friend who was to become my husband. That night we both smoked; that night, we were good friends. We had no idea that within eighteen months we would be non-smokers and all but inseparable partners.

The decision to give up was never really taken. I was unwell the week following my birthday so I didn't smoke, and when my health returned, I never really felt like having another cigarette. Since developing a closer relationship with exercise and my body, it had started to feel increasingly odd, jarring even, to have cigarettes in my life: to feel the exercise-induced burn in my lungs as they cried out for air, to feel them expand like a pair of bellows after a longer-distance run, and then to reward myself by filling them with cigarette smoke. I didn't want to do it any more, so I didn't.

Perhaps this decision was made easier because by then the

sense of exhale, of release, was occurring as an unconscious response to the deeper inhalations I was taking as I trained and became fitter. Perhaps, like my future husband, the exhale had been there all along, consistent and reliable but as yet going utterly unnoticed for what it was.

No matter how romantic this realisation was, it did not help me in my attempts to exhale in the pool. Increasingly desperate for advice, for anything that might prove to be the magic nugget of wisdom, I endlessly nagged a good friend and neighbour for inspiring hints and tips. We had known each other for years, time during which I had happily assumed he was a committed hedonist and devoted ignorer of exercise. When, to my consternation, I discovered that several times a week he would get up at the crack of dawn to knock out one hundred or more lengths in the local pool, I became convinced he would be able to impart some advice that would change things.

More fool me. The best he ever came up with was to tell me that 'the only way to swim is to swim'. You can imagine my delight. I was particularly annoyed when I realised that he was only really quoting me back at myself. The previous year, his wife had gone through a running slump, and I had encouraged her to persist, reassuring her that she would definitely feel more comfortable soon. 'The only way to run is to keep running,' I'd told her blithely. Yet it seemed impossible to translate those words to the water, even though I knew that clinging to the air – and therefore the carbon dioxide in my lungs – was effectively clinging to damaging toxins.

Another friend recommended trying to hum or shout under the water as a way of pushing the air out with active force. I gave humming a go, but it only reminded me of the years I owned a Vespa and used to drive around London singing loudly under my helmet until a bicycle courier parked next to me at a set of traffic lights pointed out that he could hear me.

I had already given shouting a try, back in the summer, when I would repeatedly attempt to swim alone under the watchful eye of the beach lifeguards. One afternoon, as I was trying to work at home, D had returned early meaning any hope of further work was over. I stomped to the beach before hurling myself into the sea. Unable to swim properly, I spent time treading water before flinging myself into brief, angry attempts at crawl, accompanied by the noise of my shouting as loud as I could under the surface. It was an unsuccessful afternoon all round.

I even confided in an old boss, who I bumped into at a work event. Inspiring and terrifying in equal measure, she had been someone I was almost too scared to speak to in my first job, fifteen years earlier. When she asked how I was, and I told her about my aquatic struggles, she surprised me by confessing to being an avid swimmer herself. Again I begged for advice. This time I thought I was on to something: she suggested that I practise the act of exhaling while not in the water itself. 'Get a washing-up bowl, put it on a table, and practise exhaling while you're seated in front it,' she advised. I went home vibrating with excitement about trying my new trick, but the glow didn't last. Maybe it was the height of the table, maybe it was the size of the washing-up bowl, but I simply couldn't replicate the sensation of putting my face into a pool, or the sea. The experience led to little more than a fresh insight into a once unknowable boss, and a lot of splashed water to clear up.

Another swimming lesson passed, and still the struggle to fully exhale continued to dog me. At first I had been trying to breathe every second stroke, consistently turning my head to the right. It wasn't working: the frequency of the breath meant there was almost no time for my much-sought-after glide. As for the idea of finding a small pocket of air in the bow wave created by my head, it was laughable. I was in almost constant flailing motion, legs tipping and head twisting, despite my arms now having a semblance of proficiency. The wave I created was not yet the luxurious, streamlined curve of a plush yacht; more a jacuzzi of panic.

Kim and Julia, who were teaching the beginners' lane, suggested that I try breathing every fourth stroke instead. Perhaps the fitness I had built up running meant that I didn't actually need to be taking in oxygen every couple of seconds, and trying every fourth stroke would give me more time to work on my body position and movement in the water, while allowing precious extra seconds to fully exhale. After all, a huge part of the problem was that I still wasn't ready to snatch an inhale when my head tilted. I promised that next week I would give it my best shot.

With a full week to acquiesce to the idea of exhaling as a positive act, I embarked on a frenzy of research. When else did my body instinctively hold on to breath, reluctant to let it go? The answer was simple: whenever I was tense. I visualised myself opening a letter that might contain important news, watching a dramatic TV show, or listening to a loved one telling me something I didn't want to hear. The stance was always the same: shoulders raised, lips pursed, sometimes even a hand to the mouth. A state of pause, everything frozen to cling on to that air. There is an inextricable link between our breathing and our psychological state.

Breathing, I learned, is controlled by the respiratory centre in the brain stem. It knows how to control our breathing rate and depth, according to the amount of carbon dioxide, oxygen and acidosis in our arterial blood (the blood being taken away from the heart, which is busy pumping fresh, oxygenated blood around the body). If carbon dioxide levels increase, for example because of exercise, the respiratory centre will be activated and our breathing rate will elevate to what it needs. Hence breathlessness when we break into a run, which steadies when we hit an even pace. We don't think about this as it's happening, though; it's an involuntary or automatic response to the situation. The magic begins the moment our umbilical cord is cut and we take our first cry; from that breath onwards we are on our own, breathing alone and unguided. Untaught and instinctive, it happens whether we want it to or not, whether we try or not, whether we are even conscious or not.

But of course, it's not that simple. There are stress hormones that also have an impact on our breathing. Adrenaline, and norepinephrine, the first guys on the scene in a moment of stress (cortisol tends to be released later, and at a slower pace), immediately change our heart rate – and therefore the rate at which we need to breathe in order to keep the blood oxygenated. They divert blood away from the gut and to our muscles so that we're ready to run away from danger, come what may.

Sometimes these moments of panic can bring on hyperventilation, the act of over-breathing caused by our body's attempts to ready itself for a danger that may never come. More often, the moment of stress can make us hold our breath. It is understood that this may be linked to our most basic responses: we hold our breath in order to be more silent, better at hiding from danger.

This instinct must have been really useful in a *Game of Thrones*-style duel scenario, or during the terrifying moment when a hungry dinosaur is listening for your anxious panting. But at the same time, it limits the amount of oxygen you're taking in, and thus the amount of oxygen in your blood, which means your heart needs to work increasingly hard in order to supply your organs with oxygen.

I wasn't convinced that learning to exhale could be achieved by the simple act of trying harder, or relaxing more, until I discovered that breathing is unique among our other visceral functions (such as digestion or endocrine) in that it can be regulated voluntarily. Our behavioural (or voluntary) control of breathing is right there in the cortex of the brain, and we can initiate it at will: for example, when we take a huge breath before singing, shouting or playing certain musical instruments. We can learn to control it consciously. Therefore, surely, I thought, we must be able to trigger the relaxation response.

And it turns out that we can. Tests have repeatedly proven that breathing exercises can have a positive impact on the blood's pH level, and can help sufferers of asthma, heart conditions and other health issues. We can train the body's response to stressful situations, and therefore its production of these stress hormones. The sympathetic nervous system is the part that creates the sensation of breathlessness in us, the same stress-induced giddiness that I felt as I entered the sea on that one-day course. What I know now, but didn't know then, is that slow, deep breathing stimulates the opposing parasympathetic nervous system, controlled by the vagus nerve, which calms us down. By taking deep, steady breaths – making sure to exhale properly – we engage the nerve, which puts the brakes on the production of those hormones that are making us breathless. You *can* use your mind to change your body.

I had to make a conscious decision to relax in order to breathe better, and breathing better would be a conscious move towards relaxing more. It seemed too good to be true. Finally, an offhand comment that Patrick had made earlier in the course made more sense. 'The minute you are thinking about swimming, you're not swimming: you're just surviving.' At the time I thought, Christ, that sounds just like how internet dating felt, but with my new-found breathing knowledge, I saw the point he was making – to reach at least a sense of proficiency, or at best a sense of pleasure or flow, we must voluntarily create an automatic response in ourselves.

Could I actively decide to relax in the water? After all, I had decided to keep running, and all it had taken was to repeat the same small movements again and again until the magic happened and they stopped feeling like torture and began to re-emerge as solace. Or, as the acting coach Constantin Stanislavski put it: 'Make the difficult habitual, the habitual easy, and the easy beautiful.' Basically: fake it till you make it.

Despite my continuing lack of style and speed in the pool, there was a sense that no matter what I experienced on the way to the water, or how badly I performed in it, the everyday wobbles that I felt on land seemed to vanish. When heavy, or exhausted, the thud of a foot and leg on tarmac or concrete is unforgiving, the jiggle visible. But over time, I was learning to trust, even love, the water's ability to hold me, making me feel weightless and streamlined, regardless of how inelegantly I moved through it.

The fact that being in water really can feel like being held reminded me of a letter I had discovered in the summer, written in the early 1760s by US founding father Benjamin Franklin to his friend Oliver Neave, who seems to have been some sort of seafaring merchant type. I hadn't been able to find out what prompted the letter, but the contents speak of 'dread', suggesting that Mr Neave was terrified of swimming – not ideal if your livelihood was so ocean-bound. Franklin goes to great lengths to encourage, telling him, 'You will be no swimmer till you can place some confidence in the power of the water to support you; I would therefore advise acquiring that confidence in the first place.' How wise he was.

He then launches into a slightly alarming description of a trust exercise involving wading into water breast deep with an egg, then turning to face the shore and throwing the egg towards it. If you leap for the egg, he insists, you will feel the water lift your legs and support you. I never worked out why the egg was so central to Franklin's trust games, but he did also invent my trusty ally the swim fin, without which I would never have got through those crucial first few lessons, so he definitely knew what he was talking about when it came to anxiety in the water.

Either way, the realisation that for hundreds of years men have been terrified of putting their faces in water made me smile. That loneliness, the moments you spend with it lapping at eye level while you try to calm your heart enough to do more than tread water and stare; they are not modern phenomena. For centuries we have felt it. But for centuries the lure of the water has been strong enough to keep tempting us forward.

To try hard to be relaxed is one of the most futile pursuits we can ever engage in. So I made myself two promises before the next week's lesson: I would take Stanislavski's advice and just keep going until the difficult was at least habitual, if not yet easy or beautiful; and I would do it visualising the most relaxing thing that I could. I would try and embody the spirit of relaxation, hoping that it would in turn convince my mind and my breathing.

Luckily for me, I saw my sister the day before that lesson. I sat with her, facing her six-month-old son as she fed him. He was without a doubt the most confident being I had ever come across. He was born sure that this was his world and we were lucky to be passing through it at the same time as him. He was, frankly, an inspiration. That week, however, he was also making the move from milk and baby rice to mashed food, and we were all invited to share his experience. Time and again my sister would carefully spoon some of the mashed sweet potato into his mouth, and he would blow out with his lush, soft lips, spraying it across his high chair, and us.

He wasn't doing it for any reason other than it felt nice. He had just discovered the different noises and vibrations of which he was master, and he was entranced by the buzzing sensation he was capable of making. As I looked at him, orange flecks in his golden-blonde eyelashes and spattered up his cheek, I realised that he was the spirit of relaxation that I needed to embody. Even his limbs were soft, floppy with contentment. Here was a guy who really knew how much fun exhaling could be: I needed to think more like Fred.

As I entered the pool the next day, I pushed my head underwater immediately and tried my soft-lipped, Fred-inspired exhale. Seconds later, I popped up smiling. It was satisfying. I felt like a child who had turned the page in a picture book and seen an image of a horse. Loose lips, relaxed exhale, I could do this. And it turned out that I could.

I started slow and steady, and kept going. Habitual, easy, beautiful, I repeated to myself, turning to breathe every four strokes. Each time I turned, I was ready to inhale: a short, sharp gasp from the side of my mouth, lips twisted like Popeye. I managed it for the entire lesson, and the next week I committed to taking it to every third breath, aiming for the holy grail of open-water swimmers: bilateral breathing. If I could master this, I would have vastly improved visibility in open water, being able to see from both sides as I took breaths, and I would be making sure that I didn't develop uneven muscle patterns across my body from breathing to only one side.

Within a fortnight, it had clicked. In forcing myself to relax enough to breathe the way I needed to, my steady breathing was relaxing me further in the water. Slowly it dawned on me that in conquering my breath I had moved a step closer to doing something else entirely: conquering my mind. It turned out that the water, the views, the sense of achievement were not the only pleasures of swimming: it was that the act of swimming itself did not create relaxation so much as demand it of you.

As spring rolled around, I discovered that – at last – when I swam, I was no longer thinking about swimming. Instead, I was, to my immense pleasure, thinking about nothing at all.

CHAPTER FIVE
From Pier to Pier

The distance from Brighton's derelict West Pier to its main pier – the Palace Pier – is less than one kilometre. Running, it's two songs' worth. Walking, it's the length of time it takes to eat an ice cream. Swimming, it represented a distance that, by spring, I could just about do in the pool. To swim that distance, from pier to pier, was the aim of the course, and to me, it now seemed just about feasible.

But the event was only a few weeks away, and there was one major stumbling block in my progress: the weather was still not stable enough for our class to start having lessons in the sea. Each week was a waiting game. I would keep an eye on weather forecasts and try to decipher tide timetables, charts and apps referencing wave height, tide and swell. As the day went on, I would nervously check my phone, waiting for the verdict. An hour before our class, the decision would be taken regarding the sea's suitability for an outdoor lesson.

This waiting, this weekly reminder of how unreliable the sea was in comparison to the land, drove me to despair. I would start my meteorological investigations the minute I woke up, anxiously checking on my new wetsuit and staring out of the window like King Canute. But the view never seemed to change: the seafront was relentlessly tormented by wind, the sea rendered a constant foamy menace, my mood similarly unsettled.

For four consecutive weeks, this stormy weather meant that our sea swimming lessons – intended to comprise the third of our three terms, were cancelled. If the weather is bad for a runner, we remind ourselves that skin is waterproof and carry on regardless. If it's bad for outdoor swimmers, you have to head for chlorinated captivity. Endless drills ensued, and as each week passed, the relief at not having to confront the sea churned in the pit of my stomach together with anxiety that if I didn't do it soon, it might be too late. Without enough practice, I wouldn't be able to do the Pier to Pier swim. Indeed, without enough practice, I might never be able to swim in the sea at all.

Instead, and with a looming sense of dread, I focused on hitting the goal of being able to swim non-stop for an hour. This, I understood, was the longest the swim could possibly take, if the tide and wind were against us. Perhaps we would get lucky and it would take half that, but we couldn't know until the day itself. I knew that one thing I could do to control the outcome was to get myself fit enough, so I would turn up to the pool every week and take part in drills focused on getting us ready to cope in open water. We would do batches of ten or twenty lengths concentrating on different skills – our kick, our catch, our push and our pull. We would try and use one breath for as many strokes as possible – first three, then five, then seven, and nine if we could manage it. Then there would be sprints, and recovery lengths, and more sprints.

What I hadn't appreciated in all of this training was that every few lengths I had the chance to stand at the shallow end, adjusting my goggles and steadying my breath. This was brought to my attention a couple of weeks before the class finally moved into the sea, when we were told that instead of touching the end and kicking off each time, we had to keep swimming and turn without contact with the pool wall, treading water instead. The difference in effort required seemed huge, and once again I felt those creeping tentacles of anxiety reaching for me.

The other step I knew I could take was to try and get myself accustomed to, if not comfortable with, the sensation of cold water on my body. The air temperature itself was by now not too bad: a muggy if blustery May. As for the water, I had no idea. There was only one real solution, and it in turn led to one of my great swimming passions: the lido.

The pool where my lido love began was, strictly speaking, built too early to be deemed a lido – a term that only really caught on in the 1930s. The Pells Pool in Lewes is tucked into a hilly corner of this sleepy Sussex town, about a twenty-minute drive from Brighton. Built in 1860, it is the oldest freshwater swimming pool in the country, Grade II listed, and quite possibly heaven. When I heard whispers (via lane-end chat at the indoor pool) of a group of swimmers who had hired the Pells Pool one evening a week purely for lane swimming practice, I was consumed with jealousy. When I discovered that Alan, another beginner who I had been following up and down the pool since September, was one of them, I was most excited. And when I was invited to come along one Monday night, I may as well have been invited to join the Bilderberg Group.

We drove up on a close, sunny evening, the sort of weather where light, pollen and noise hang in the air as if waiting to be told their next move. In contrast to the seafront in Brighton, where by this time of year tourists, seagulls and crashing waves all compete for sonic supremacy, the approach to the Pells was all but silent. The seafront gusts were gone, left behind on the other side of the Sussex Downs, and the air was swollen with a slow restfulness.

The pool, fed with spring water from beneath the land, is huge – 150 feet long and half as wide. And, crucially, it's entirely unheated. After lowering myself into the chilly but not cold water, I treated myself to a bit of breaststroke and a chance to get my bearings for the first length or so. I quickly learned that the bottom of the pool curves where it meets the ends, making if feel almost bath-like as you ready yourself to turn.

The water itself is surrounded by an expanse of grass, alongside which is a small children's paddling pool, and the entire area is walled with Victorian red brick. The cluster of Corsican pine trees at one end, dotted with the occasionally chirruping blackbird, gives the impression that the pool might just be an oasis in the middle of a forest. At the entrance is a fabulously anachronistic kiosk, dating back to the 1961 centenary celebrations, its sky-blue, white and red frontage managing to both jar with and complement the rest of the Victorian splendour.

I put my head down and got on with the business of some front-crawl training. At nearly fifty metres, the pool was more than twice as big as any I had trained in before. Twice the size meant half the breaks, so at first I struggled to keep myself going before at last falling into a steady rhythm. For lap upon lap I was struck by the fresh taste of the water. Filtered rather than cleaned with chlorine, it could have been poured straight from a glass bottle. After long, wintry months of chlorine making me sneeze all the way home after an indoor swim, and the still vivid memory of salt water's abrasive drag on the back of my nose and throat, this was delicious.

The overall effect was one of taking a dip in both history and nature. I was aware that this was a pool that had served the town for over 150 years. Here, Victorian workers washed themselves before and after shifts, Second World War soldiers trained for battle, and generations of local children were taught to swim. It was not until 1936 that the pool started to be referred to as a lido, five years after the segregation of the sexes ceased to be enforced (until 1931, women and girls were only permitted at the pool two mornings a week). Around this time, the iconic changing cubicles with their primary-coloured doors – now familiar from movies and photo shoots – were installed.

As I turned my head to breathe, I could see not the sides of an indoor pool, with its safety notices and harsh strip lamps, but evening sun dappling between the trees above. I could smell the freshly cut grass only metres away, I could taste the spring below me in the earth itself, and I could hear the blackbirds flitting from tree to tree over my head. If this was outdoor swimming, I was a convert for life.

Trips to the Pells became – and remain – a summertime weekly occurrence, but between those Monday evening swims I began to venture further afield. When I went to London to visit my siblings, both of whom lived in Tooting, I was introduced to the delights of Tooting Bec Lido. Ambitiously named the Tooting Bathing-Lake on being completed in 1906, it is almost double the size of the Pells Pool, and is the largest outdoor freshwater pool in the country. Truly, at nearly twice Olympic size, it is startlingly enormous. Another tree-lined haven, it is only metres from the roar of the traffic hurtling alongside Tooting Common, but still manages to feel like a calm micro-universe tucked away from whatever else South London might be busying itself with.

In the sea, the push and pull of the waves, as well as the movement of tides or currents beneath you, is always audible. In an indoor pool, the proximity of the walls to the water creates an echo effect that amplifies every splash, clang or playful shriek. In an outdoor lido, however, sounds seem to vanish. When I asked a sound engineer friend if this was actually possible, or if it was just my emotional response to calm recreational spaces, he confirmed that it was not merely my overactive imagination: the absence of close, high walls lets sound drift further and therefore seem quieter. The roar of the breath beneath the water remains the same, but the roar of nearby traffic shrinks away.

How had I been missing out on these urban oases for so long? I chose not to dwell on the answer, but to focus on the new opportunities available to me. Where once I would head to a café or amble around the shops if I had a gap between meetings in London, I started to pack a towel and swimming costume instead. For those few weeks I roamed all over the city, like a twenty-first-century version of John Cheever's Neddy Merrill, albeit one less boozy and considerably less scornful of public pools.

Indeed, it is the very public nature of these pools and lidos of the late nineteenth and early twentieth centuries that I find so inspiring. Sure, there are some magnificent hotel pools and some truly slick private membership club pools liberally scattered across the capital, and indeed the country. But it is these lido gems that truly capture our imagination. Once liberated from the petty confines of gender segregation nearly one hundred years ago, and unencumbered by the dangerous, cloying legacy of racial segregation of so many US public pools – decades worth of black children not being allowed to swim, leading to a further generation of black children afraid of the water – our lidos are truly civic spaces. The more I saw of them that summer, the more I understood that they are not just for exercise or relaxation, but, crucially, serve as vital opportunities to witness that infinite variety and fortitude of bodies that walk – or swim – among us. To be lapped by a grandmother, to be watched by a curious child, to be asked to help at the steps by someone infirm on land and as buoyant as a baby in the water – this, I came to learn, was just as important a part of being a swimmer as training for an event ever can be.

Because however exposing the act of getting to the water in nothing but a swimming costume may be, the communities that swimmers have built truly cement my faith in human nature. In Brighton there is a group, promoted and supported by the council, for trans swimmers. In London, the Swim Dem Crew specifically tries to encourage those who would not normally get into the water to do so. All over the country there are children finding their confidence in the water thanks to swimming being part of the national curriculum.

The more I chatted to the lifeguards or my fellow swimmers, the more I realised how beloved these lidos are. When the state cannot or will not fund them, local communities rally time and time again to keep them open. Tooting Bec Lido is run by the South London Swimming Club during the winter months, when only the hardy and experienced want to swim. Rockwell Lido was closed in 1990 before a campaign was initiated to save it, reopening it in 1994. In 1999, the Pells Pool was saved under similar circumstances, and as I write, six miles away on the other side of Brighton, Saltdean Lido is being prepared for its 2017 reopening, a community interest company having bought it from the council.

We want our public pools – particularly our outdoor pools – to reflect our better, calmer nature, to encourage in wider society the sense of peace and restfulness that we experience while there. And thus far, we are doing a great job. They should be treasured, every single one.

Finally, nearly ten months after that first fateful attempt, the weather cleared, and the wind dropped: it was time to get back into the sea. I was strong enough, I was prepared enough, and I was trusted enough. But still, on the morning of that first outdoor lesson, I got myself into such a sweat that it took me nearly half an hour to yank my wetsuit on. Eventually I was in, and headed out for the only-slightly-mortifying walk to the spot on the beach where the class was due to meet.

It was exactly where the one-day course had taken place, to the east of the Palace Pier, and it was another glorious day. After a mild but grey start to the summer, the sunlight felt dazzling, as if the ceiling on the world had been lifted a few hundred feet, and with it my confidence. The sky above the clouds was revealed! And so would my new self be: a sea swimmer!

The group was gathered on the pebbles by the time I arrived, and we were given a briefing about the conditions and reminded to do our acclimatisation exercise. 'Exhale. Get all the air out before you try and swim,' said James, who was manning the safety kayak. Moments later, I waded confidently in; only this time I knew the value of the acclimatisation and exhalations. I happily dunked my head into the water, and despite every instinct wanting to clasp my breath within me, I breathed out. I really, really breathed out, forcing everything I could from my lungs. I felt the cold reach my hairline, and into my wetsuit, but I kept going, pushing, exhaling, until I had completed five deep breaths. So far, so good.

The three temporary swimming buoys were once again positioned about fifty metres apart in the water, and our task was to get our bearings and swim between them. For now, my breathing was calm and I was bobbing, treading water, at a depth where I could still feel the bottom. A few feet further, and I knew the pebbly shelf would give way sharply beneath me. Brighton doesn't do slow, Caribbean plateaus of sand: there are pebbles, there is a drop, and then there is deep sea. I waded forward, ready and prepared for it. But as I pushed my feet against those last few inches and lifted my legs, I suffered a sort of terrifying vertigo.

The sea wasn't too rough for me, and I knew I could swim, but I was utterly overwhelmed by being back in the ocean.

'I feel ... so out of my depth,' I heard myself mutter, understanding the expression for the first time with infuriating clarity.

Away from the pools and lidos I was now so in love with, and their regular, familiar walls, the sea seemed impossibly unknowable. There was just so much of it, and I was so tiny. The panoramic view of the shoreline that had given me unparalleled delight a year ago now seemed to be rushing at me and then away, focus zooming in and out at terrifying speed, as if Hitchcock himself were directing my anxieties for maximum effect. If I turned away from shore to face the water, the same thing happened but exponentially worse. The sea went on for ever! The endless churning movement felt like the very worst of being in an angry crowd, pushed and rocked by forces way beyond my reach. This was the acute loneliness of being a tiny body submerged in an enormous stretch of water.

But of course I wasn't alone. I was surrounded by friends, classmates and properly qualified instructors. None of whom I wanted to let down. So I smiled, trod water and fiddled with my goggles, pretending that all was well. I was less able to pretend when we were instructed to start swimming, barely able to do more than five or six strokes without bobbing back up to look around me, both horrified and mesmerised by what I could see. In hindsight, the teachers had seen all this before; they knew I had a history of panic in the open water, and they were keeping an eye on me – trusty Kim and her kayak were never far away. But in those first few moments, I felt a crushing sense of defeat I had never known with running. No matter how steep a hill, how muddy a track or how long a run, I had always known I could just walk – I could walk away and survive. But that lunchtime, I felt like I was having to wrestle with mortality itself.

I kept going, though. Trying to do my six strokes at a time before looking around to check my bearings. Each time I stopped, I felt that my breath had become short and snatched, and made a conscious effort to slow it with deep exhales. I carried on, round the buoys, slower than the others but still going, still chipping away at the terrors. I swallowed gallons; my eyes stung from the salt that snuck around the sides of my goggles and splashed my face every time I adjusted them; and the fight with my breath left me as tired as if I'd taken a sprint session on a running track. At the end of the class, I fell out of the sea, thighs bruised by the pebbles I hurled myself onto, confidence bruised by not having managed to put what I knew I should do into any sort of coherent practice.

We sat drinking coffee from a flask in the sunlight. Viewed from the beach, the sea seemed slyly innocent. I let myself believe that next week it would be easier. But it wasn't. If anything, it was harder. And the third week wasn't much better.

It took until the fourth outdoor class for something to click, whether it was confidence or experience I'll never truly know. I like to tell myself that it was those extra weeks of training I did, heading alone day after day to lane swimming sessions all over the south-east, swimming laps for an hour at a time, forcing my body to believe that it was doable, that I had the physical strength if not the mental grit. I suspect the truth is somewhat simpler: that fourth week, I could see the bottom.

It was now June, and Brighton was enjoying one of its magical days, where the sea is calm but visibly moving, every ripple looking like a seam of diamonds on a cape of blue velvet. And the tide was low. So low. We began the class with the usual briefing on the beach, but this time it took longer than I'd ever known to get to the water's edge. That shelf that had unnerved me two weeks previously was now visible, metres from the shore and bone dry. We had to clamber down it, the soles of our feet pressing pebbles and feeling for flatness among them to keep ourselves upright.

Even when we hit the water, it took a further thirty metres or so of wading to get even close to chest deep, and most of that was done on cashmere-soft sand, through clear blue water. By the time we reached the buoys, I had half convinced myself I was on a summer holiday. I was giddy with joy at the conditions, actually looking forward to tipping my face in and giving it a go.

And when I did, it was heaven. My mind, clear of anxiety because I knew I could both see and touch the ocean floor, let my body do its own thing. I naturally exhaled, no part of my subconscious urging me to cling on to carbon dioxide-filled air that I didn't need. Consequently I felt smoother in the water and moved more easily. I recognised that those first minutes of swimming were my body warming up, not an inability to swim properly. Before long, my lungs and arms were moving in synch, just as I knew they could in the pool. We were not following buoys this time, but swimming parallel to the beach. I let my eyes rest. Instead of searching for danger in the murky water, they could clearly follow the sandy floor and its hundreds of tiny shells and rivulets of water dancing around below me. I let the gentle movement of the sea rock me, able to sense for the first time when motion was incoming and where I might need to alter my head position a little to breathe. Above all, I let myself swim.

Once I was actually swimming – continuously, in the sea! – it seemed so simple. I could have been doing it for weeks, if I had only let myself believe. Instead, I had allowed my mind to squat in a mess of self-doubt and baseless anxiety. I knew enough about my own fitness levels to be aware that I wasn't that much fitter than I had been a month ago. It wasn't a muscle I had needed to flex, but my brain. By simply being able to see the sandy floor, I had let my mind relax, my body flood with delicious fresh oxygen, and my body follow, doing what I had now long known was within my grasp.

My instinct was to chastise myself for being the one holding back my progress. But what would that have achieved? I had swum! Exhausted, I whooped, clinked paper coffee cups with my classmates and headed home feeling infallible. By the time of my first event, I would be positively amphibian!

The truth was not quite that magnificent, but relative to my previous performances, the Pier to Pier swim was a triumph indeed. It was a calm, sunny evening, and the beach was littered with couples and gaggles of friends having barbecues, fishing for mackerel, or just enjoying a beer as they waited for sunset. Seagulls were squawking, children were prancing and music was playing. It was the sort of scene that regularly prompts D to comment how 'Brighton is looking very "first half-hour of *Jaws*" tonight'. The water was dotted with jet-skiers and paddle-boarders, but mercifully no windsurfers. The conditions were good.

We met on the beach opposite the remains of the West Pier, a huddle of about twelve or fifteen of us, and had a security briefing reminding us not to let ourselves get dragged west into the rubble of rotting iron that made up the remains of the decaying structure. Similarly, we were warned against the tide dragging us towards the forest of iron supports still standing at the base of the Palace Pier. The same safety kayak that I had clung to in despair eleven months previously was launched into the sea, ready to keep an eye on us, and behind it we waded out until the water was deep enough for us to start to swim.

And, with a simple catch, pull, push, I swam. I knew that D was waiting with my towel and kit at the Palace Pier, and I knew that if I could do this swim, I would have effectively graduated from the course that had meant so much to me all year. Yet with each stroke, the idea of graduating became less and less important. As I felt the water supporting me, and saw the sun glinting benignly whenever I tipped my gaze for breath, I understood that what the course had done for me was to unlock the door to an other-worldly set of experiences. Already, for some weeks, I'd had the key; now the door was open, and I was a swimmer.

I reached the Palace Pier and was back in D's arms within half an hour. We wandered home along the seafront together, me in a daze of satisfaction and D keeping quiet enough to suggest that he probably could have done this swim without a year of training and drama. I didn't care how easy anyone else might have found it, though. The mission had been mine. And now it was complete. Luckily, I had another one right around the corner.

CHAPTER SIX
Down the River

What possessed me to enter an event that was four times the length of that one-kilometre swim from pier to pier, and what possessed me to do it for my first formal open-water swim remain two of my more mysterious decisions.

Perhaps it was that, when my breathing finally clicked and I could swim for stretches of about twenty minutes at a time, I had a little burst of confidence, which sent me something close to delirious when contemplating what else I could do now that I was relaxed in the water. Perhaps it was simply the excitement of getting to the Palace Pier that day. Perhaps it was just curiosity.

Either way, surviving was no longer enough; I wanted to be able to taste all that swimming had to offer me. I could handle 3.8 kilometres down a river I had never seen before in my life. But as the bubble of confidence and overexcitement popped, I realised the weight of what I had taken on. I might be able to do an hour in a lido, but I hadn't been in the sea for more than half an hour in my life. And I had never swum in a river at all.

The event was to take place down the River Arun, in West Sussex, towards the small seaside town of Littlehampton.

Several others from my course had completed it the year before and were planning to do it again. I tried to ignore the fact that they were all more experienced swimmers who had been training in different lanes to the one I had learned in over the last few months.

'If you can swim confidently for an hour, you'll be fine,' they said to me at the final swimming class of the term. 'The current will do the rest.'

I liked the sound of that, even if I wasn't entirely sure it was true. But as the fee for entering the event was significantly less than the increasingly prohibitive cost of entering running events, I decided to buy myself a place and see how I felt nearer the time. I quietly told D that we were going to the beach in Littlehampton that day, wrote words to that effect in our shared calendar, and busied myself with my new schedule of fretting. And what a busy schedule it was.

I would think about the eerie, reedy tendrils that I'd seen on the edge of rivers, ready to brush against legs. I would wonder what river water tasted like. I would fret about what to pack for such an event. I thought about all those things constantly, and would sit up with a start in bed, muttering non sequiturs such as: 'What if you get thirsty but can't drink the river water?' just as D was falling asleep.

I would ask what I could at swimming classes, quickly, before we all had to dash back to work or children, but my questions were usually random and useless, rather than the sensible ones I would remember at three o'clock in the morning and promise myself I'd ask the next week. I tried to remember what I found useful for a half-marathon, and apply it to a swimming event. But it didn't always work. I knew that if it was rainy before a running event, you could cover yourself in a black bin bag and the organisers would generally be prepared for those taking part to strip them off, along with some old second-hand sweats, just before the starting gun fired. But how ready were you supposed to be when you arrived for a swimming event? Surely there weren't changing areas for all the participants? Should you wear your wetsuit there? Or be happy to put it on, over your swimsuit, in public? I was barely comfortable walking along Brighton beach with my wetsuit half on and a towel round my shoulders – how would that work out in the centre of Littlehampton?

Were there facilities for kit bags, as there are at running events? What happened in case of emergency? I had always had my phone at running events; I had even had a tiny Nokia during my first marathon, which took place before the advent of smartphones. This time I would be uncontactable from the moment I left for the start, which was miles upriver. How would that feel? And how did these events start anyway? Were they true, those tales I had heard online of broken ribs and kicks in the face as swimmers fought for space? How did you know how far you had swum and how far you had to go? Were there the equivalent of mile markers anywhere? Or a drinks station?

Admittedly, some of the answers to these queries were readily available on the event's website, but others remained unanswered until the day of the swim itself.

The day, when it arrived, was inauspicious. It was not windy, but the sky was smothered in the sort of low, dirty cloud that makes looking up feel as if you're trying to peek out from a piece of scummy old Tupperware . It was far from the sort of morning where dreams are realised. I did not want to go at all.

The only thing that kept me from shirking altogether was the memory of a conversation I'd had with my sister a few weeks earlier, when I had told her that I wanted to swim this river event, and then head to Greece in order to swim to Ithaca.

'Why do you do all this?' she had asked me. 'What's the end point?'

I shrugged her off at the time, getting away with a flippant 'Because I can', but the real answer wasn't far off.

I wanted to swim out there in the rivers and lakes and oceans because it felt like developing a superpower, an extra part of a self I had believed to be static, or at least limited. Over the course of the year, as the stroke and the breathing and the sense of peace I had come to feel in the water had developed, it was almost as if I'd learned to fly. By this point, when I dreamt that I was flying (which I do about once a month), even the position of my arms had changed to something more like a swimmer's stroke, instead of the wide-open wings of a bird. Freedom takes on a different shape once you're a swimmer.

To discover a new skill as an adult is like noticing a door, deciding to open it and finding an entire room in your own home that you never knew you had. And I had done it – I had opened the door to the extra room. Now I wanted to be able to see water, anywhere in the world – oceans, lakes and pools – and sense not fear but adventure and peace.

Because a life lived most fully is not the one with the most money earned, the most stuff bought or the most races won, but the one with the most experiences experienced the most fully. I wanted to dive into water as I wanted to dive into life: filled with joy, curiosity, and the knowledge that though there might be dangers, they aren't daunting enough to make it not worth doing. And by the grotty morning of that river swim, those feelings were within touching distance.

D had, by now, accepted the new superhero status that I had bestowed upon the act of swimming down a river with the current on my side. I had explained the true nature of our trip to Littlehampton and he had dealt with it with admirable serenity. Having had his support over the course of several marathons, either as friend or partner, in person or via text, tweet and even FaceTime, I knew that he made an honourable backup crew, however sanguine he might be during the hours before the event.

So he was with me on the train that unpromising morning. It was early, and quiet, and there was no sign of any other swimmers. I rooted around in my rucksack, checking and rechecking that I had with me what I thought I'd need: my wetsuit, my goggles, the coloured cap that had been sent to me as evidence of my entry into the event, a large tube of moisturiser, my flip-flops. Occasionally I would bleat randomly:

'I don't even know where the start line is – it's just a blob on my phone map.'

'Will I see an actual fish?'

'How do we get out afterwards?'

'Will you be there at the end? Cheering?'

'Just stay calm,' he said. 'Don't waste your energy on what might happen, but look out for things you *know* will happen. You know you'll have to breathe right. You know you'll see your hands in the water every time you take a stroke. You know not to kick too hard. You know all of that.'

We worked on the list of knowns for a while during that thirty-minute train ride. But the one comment that really stuck in my mind was one that was entirely useless: 'I'll tell you what else I know. There's always a tattoo parlour with a funny name near the station in towns this size.'

When we arrived in Littlehampton, I checked in at the makeshift desk in the RNLI boat shed, which was headquarters for the event. A marker pen was used to write my competitor number on my hands. 'Just in case!' said the woman behind the desk, with a cheery smile. One I did not return. To her left was a second desk, where we were invited to leave bags if we wanted to. My trusty support crew offered to take care of mine.

Outside the boat shed was a large concrete ramp where they launched the lifeboats, which headed either left (out to sea, and Littlehampton beach), or right (up the river). This was where we would finish the race. On the ramp were several swans. Huge, confident swans, picture-book examples of the vicious beasts that primary school children are warned about. Unsurprisingly, for birds that revel in the knowledge that they could break your arm if they wanted to, they seemed unperturbed by the increasing number of people clustering nearby. Theirs was the strut of animals who know they look good, know they swim well, and know they will get the river back to themselves before too long. It was also a strut that I would have to walk alongside if I was planning to get out of the river in an hour or two's time. My stomach tightened, as did D's hand in mine.

Outdoor swimming events are not new – people have been racing on the Thames since Victorian times, swimming across Lake Windermere since the 1920s and taking part in triathlons for decades. But they were new to me. And I had no idea what I was letting myself in for. I had managed to grasp snatches of information from my classmates, but it's hard to really express how anxious you are when you're wrapped in a towel and your hair is dripping on their shoes.

Our early arrival meant we had time to spare, so we headed into the RNLI café for a cup of tea. At this point I was wearing my swimming costume underneath leggings and a sweatshirt, and had my wetsuit and goggles in my swimming rucksack with my towel and change of clothes. It did not take long to realise how desperately inadequate this was as a look. I may as well have turned up in a swimsuit to the Oscars. As every minute passed, more and more men (and a few women) arrived in their boldly emblazoned triathlon club kits, shaking hands and indulging in bracing, deeply masculine slaps on the back.

These were not professional athletes. They were largely middle-aged men. But they were all decked out in the kind of kit I associated with the opening ceremonies of international sporting events. Branded hoodies, branded bags and branded 'event wear' was dripping off every last one of them. And I could tell – from the extensive wetsuit research I had done before buying a second-hand one – that they were all wearing top-of-the-range neoprene as well. I felt like the high-school dweeb at a party for jocks.

I am used to being patronised, underestimated and even physically pushed out of the way by a very distinct type of sporty bloke. Almost always white, almost always over thirty-five and almost always confident that they know more about sport than me. This crowd were not entirely new to me when they started to emerge that Saturday morning. They don't mean to be rude, I sincerely believe that. They are merely vibrating with the sort of fragile masculinity that means their identity is closely tethered to how fast they can run, swim or cycle.

I don't know if they realise how intimidating they can be. Is it part of the warm-up to throw yourself around, flashing your expensive kit and thwacking passing strangers in the eye with a flick of your rucksack? Or is it how their nerves manifest themselves – sticking in tiny groups, talking louder than necessary and standing or sitting with legs spread obnoxiously? Either way, they make me sad. Not for myself, as I was lucky enough to have my dad and my brother on side from the second I invested a millisecond in exercise. They let me know that this behaviour is no shorthand for sportiness; that it really is just rudeness. But what if I hadn't had my family when I started? Would I have been one of the very many women who now tell me, regularly, that they are too intimidated to enter sporting events because they're not the right type of person? I like to think not, but I am far from sure.

It seemed that the loveliness of my classmates and the open, non-judgemental, welcoming environment of my swimming course had lulled me into a false sense of security about what kind of person might be at a formal swimming event. I had hoped for something gentler, but had not realised that because the swim was the same distance as an Ironman one, it might be filled with competitive amateur sportsmen at their most objectionable, as well as those who simply liked swimming in rivers. I'm sure they're all charming when they're not in neoprene, I told myself as I cast my gaze across the cliques.

'Stay cool,' said D, who had done well to recognise that muscle clenching just below my temple. I winked at him as I went to the bathroom to put on my wetsuit. I will spare you the details of how well that went. Suffice to say the cubicles were less than roomy.

The energy in the café had changed when I emerged, and people were starting to move from their tables and gather their kit before heading for the coaches. I took a deep breath and braced myself to do the same. It was only now, as I bent down to pack my sweatshirt into my rucksack on the floor, and saw a pair of gnarly bare feet centimetres from my face, that I realised I had to surrender my footwear. The alternative was to face losing them at a riverbank several kilometres away. How had I not thought of this before? How had I not realised that if we were being bussed from the finish to the start line, we could take nothing at all with us?

Forgive me, I'm aware that it seems princessy, and that there are many, many people with greater problems, but having wet or dirty feet horrifies me. It's not so much the thought of actual dirt, but the squelch of not walking on dry land makes my stomach heave the way that some people respond to the sound of nails being dragged down a blackboard, or someone eating a banana on a train, or baby sick over a parent's shoulder. For me it is, and always has been, the potential for the slippery and the gooey that quickens my heart rate to a state of appalled panic.

I would rather spend five years running marathons – a world of blisters and pain – than walk to the side of a swimming pool without my flip-flops. In gyms and swimming pools, my foot is removed from its sock and placed directly into the flip-flop. The possibility of it coming into contact with damp balls of fluff from other people's clothes, or clumps of their hair, or remnants of their discarded plasters makes me want to weep like a Sicilian widow at the funeral of the most handsome man in the village.

As far as I'm concerned, the five worst foot feelings of all time are:

1) Wearing clean, fresh socks and treading in a spill.

2) Stepping barefoot on either a slimy rock in shallow seawater or an unexpectedly reedy riverbank.

3) Wearing leather summer sandals in a thunderstorm, resulting in clammy damp feet for the rest of the day as the leather slowly dries beneath your soles.

4) Walking through a swimming pool or gym changing room barefoot and feeling the fizzing of a new verruca.

5) Experiencing a night of passion, only to realise, as your foot hits the offending article, that you shared that passion with the sort of monster who would leave a condom on the floor by the bed.

All of these things are worse than the time two of my toenails fell off. You can't appreciate how horrific this ordeal is unless it has happened to you. So you can imagine my dread as the moment to board the coach barefoot suddenly roared towards me. And it wasn't just the bare feet that were the problem: I had to leave my husband, and with him our means of communication. I felt very alone. I wanted to weep, I wanted to vomit, I wanted to flee.

But I also wanted to feel the river water between my fingers, to experience the liberty of swimming in nature, away from the confines of the pool, to sense the motion of the water helping me along as I headed towards the sea. I wanted those things so much. I wanted them much more than I wanted to flee. So I had to take my shoes off and get on with it.

Having surrendered my rucksack, including my phone and shoes, to D, I boarded a decommissioned school bus. As we left the car park and drove slowly through Littlehampton, I watched the shops and cafés slide past the window. When I caught sight of what looked like a poster advertising tattooists' work, I snapped my head back as the bus moved past, trying to catch the name of the shop. D had been right: *Needle and Fred*. I looked down into my lap and smiled to myself.

Eventually the bus pulled into the car park of a small rural church. There was no river in sight, and the small gravelled area was surrounded by fields. I stepped gingerly towards the coach door, thinking serene thoughts about my vagus nerve. A slow line of wetsuits was walking barefoot around the edge of the car park to avoid the gravel, and gathering to the side of the church. I hopped as deftly as I could on to the grass behind them and joined the snaking procession. While trying not to think about snakes.

People were starting to put on their hats and goggles, and many were rolling what looked like deodorant around the edges of their wetsuits. I was curious, before surmising that it was some sort of lubricant to stop the suits from rubbing. These people with accessories seemed to have support cars that had followed them to the car park. I wondered whether I really needed lubricant, or whether it was all part of the intimidation ritual that some of the competitors seemed intent on indulging in.

Before long, the second coach arrived, and now the volume of swimmers and the number of black wetsuits and covered heads meant it was all but impossible to tell people apart. I was scanning faces frenetically, trying to find someone I recognised. Most of us looked like portly upright ants. Eventually, after much searching, I found a couple of women from my class. It was their second year doing the event, so I was almost tearfully grateful to see them.

'What happens at the start?' I asked anxiously. 'Will they swim over me?'

'Do you care about your time?' one of them asked.

'No! Of course not! I just want to make it to the end!'

'Then start at the back with us,' the other said. 'The river is wide enough that you can overtake people later if you need to.'

My shoulders instantly dropped an inch. I didn't have to join in the melee of competitive swimmers. I could do things my way.

Soon the swimmers started to move around the side of the churchyard, down a small country lane that I hadn't even spotted. We walked for about five hundred metres alongside a field of rape, each step in squelching mud. I stared at my feet, remembering childhood tantrums over muddy toes on country walks, or soggy sandals on summer trips. No matter what else happened today, I had already confronted one enormous, lifelong terror.

The three of us happily let others pass as we arrived at the river. At this point it was about a hundred metres wide. There were small buoys in place, marking the start line, just ahead of where people were entering the water, and several safety kayaks either side of them. People in swimming caps that demarcated them as aiming for faster times than us were already jostling at the front, treading water, waiting for the starting klaxon. We remained on the edge, happy to get in once the rush had passed. There were none of the pens, barriers or organisation of the large running events I had done, and none of the gentle entry procedure of our few swimming lessons in the sea.

The klaxon sounded and the river became thick with foam as the swimmers started to move. A childhood visit to the zoo, where we saw vegetables thrown into the piranha tank, surfaced in my memory. The agitated water, the sense of frenzy, the anxiety about wanting to look but being scared of what I might see. Eventually there was enough space for us to step down into the water ourselves. I forced myself to breathe as I felt the silt beneath me, the cold of the water around me, and the endless air above. Still your breath, still your mind, I told myself, and soon we were off, into the foaming water the others had left behind.

For the first ten minutes or so, I was lost in a sensory wonderland, absolutely distracted from my breath as I warmed up and found a rhythm in the water. There was none of the noise of crashing waves that I had become accustomed to in the sea, nor was I rocked from side to side by tidal swells. Breathing was significantly easier; there was air whenever I turned my head. The water was greener than I had ever seen in the sea. It was the colour and opacity of a piece of glass, washed up, jewel-like, on the shore. With every stroke I took, I could clearly see the waxy red of my nail polish dancing through the green of the water, a thousand tiny bubbles in its wake each time. It was mesmerising, almost Christmassy.

The water tasted like nothing I had experienced before. There was no salt, despite us being so close to the sea. It was exactly what I would have imagined this shade of earthy green to taste like. 'Mint and mud', Virginia Woolf called it, and I understood in those moments what she meant. It was silty, but fresh, calling to mind the chlorophyll intensity of spirulina or similarly verdant powders so beloved of health food shops. There was nothing of the familiar chlorine burn in my nose, nor the sting of salt on my lips or eyes. It was fresh.

I smiled to myself, remembering a conversation I'd had with Patrick in the week leading up to the event.

'One of the things you'll notice after all this sea swimming is the cinnamon,' he told me, as I questioned him for the umpteenth time about what it felt like to swim in a river.

'Why is that?' I queried, intrigued by this exotic nugget of information. 'What is in the earth in Sussex that could do that to the taste of water? Or does it come from the sea?'

'That's just what rivers taste like,' he said with a shrug. 'Especially after the stormy spring we've had.'

I was mystified. It was only when I relayed the entire conversation to D later that evening that he pointed out that Patrick had probably said 'sediment' rather than 'cinnamon'. Ah.

I daydreamed about this former self, the one who had never tasted a river, and after ten minutes or so I looked up, trying to get my bearings. The river was wider than I had expected, much wider than it was in Littlehampton, and the three of us, swimming at a similar pace, were taking wide zigzags rather than staying tight to its curves. I had never seen a river this wide from within. The banks seemed high and inaccessible, whereas we were low, eyes at water level, seeing the world as a duckling might. Like them, I was unable to fly, making our sunken position between the banks an inescapable one. The only way out of the river was to finish the course. There were kayaks within view, but no markers to demonstrate how far we had swum or how far we had to go. And as the route had several curves to it, there was no chance of seeing our final destination yet. I steadied my breath, chose a tree in the distance, and told the others I was aiming for that then planning to take another pause to get my bearings.

And so we continued. Swimming for ten or twelve minutes at a stretch; pausing to right our course, checking that we were all still feeling strong, then onwards. I had swum for an hour continuously in the pool, but it had always been punctuated by pauses in the shallow end. I had at least practised in open water by now, if only for about fifteen minutes of continuous swimming. But this was unlike anything I had ever experienced: we were inaccessible, plunged into nature, swimming our way home.

A beat started to form as I felt my stroke lengthen and become more confident. My breath, my body, my surroundings. We passed under bridges. We swam alongside curious swans. And I'm sure we passed over more than a few fish. All the while, there was a terrible freedom in not knowing how far I had come and how far I still had to go. Every marathon, every half-marathon, even every 5K training run, had been dictated for so long by pace, time and goals. Now, I had no idea. I knew that I wanted to be swimming, I knew I was swimming, and so I swam. On and on. Exhalation, exhilaration, exhaustion.

This, I suspected, was as close to the state of flow as I had ever felt. I had done long training runs in the past where time had appeared to pass with some elasticity, so complete was my absorption in what I was doing. But this was entirely new sensory territory. With almost nothing to look at beyond my hands' repeated motions and the bubbles they were creating, nothing to hear except the roaring of the water being forced forward by my exhalations, and nothing to taste other than the river itself, my senses seemed to reach a deep state of relaxation.

When I had first moved to Brighton, I'd been transfixed for months by the horizon, finding an enormous sense of rest in seeing the curve of the earth every day after nearly fifteen years in a dense urban environment, increasingly surrounded by screens, walls and endless moving detail. I became convinced my eyeballs were happier – not just my sense of well-being, but my actual eyeballs. When I visited the optician, she confirmed that I was right. When you are always looking at things close to you, the muscles behind your eyes are in a state of almost permanent contraction. By looking into the distance, day after day, those muscles relax; hence the sense that my eyes themselves were happier in their new home. Now, as my eyes had nothing at all to stare at, and my other senses were receiving similarly uncomplicated messages, something inside of me unfurled and let go.

This sense of contentment was unshakeable. I tried to worry – how much further did we have to go? How much more tired might I become? – but the rhythm of the river kept my heart rate steady. Just as I felt the tiredness creeping to the tips of my fingers, and starting to dull my legs, something remarkable happened: the river sped up beneath me. So this was the magical current I had been told about. I was reaching, catching, pulling the water, but somehow each stroke was taking me further than ever before. Even when I paused and looked up, still I moved forward, strong and smooth. As if it knew that I was starting to fade, the river was helping me out. All those flying dreams where my arms were in front-crawl position seemed to be coming to life.

I heard shouting from the riverbank. 'Don't miss the exit!' A man in a high-visibility jacket was waving at our group. 'Just under the red bridge now!'

I looked ahead. The red bridge was only a few hundred metres away! I recognised it from the walk from the train station. The man, I now realised, had been shouting because the river was moving so fast, we might swim straight past and head out to sea.

'I'm still feeling strong, I'm going to keep going at this pace!' I said to my companions, who were now slightly behind me. They waved me on, grinning, and I headed for the bridge. The mass of swimmers had thinned out now, and we were spaced about ten metres apart. I found strength in my arms, legs and lungs as the bridge swooped above me and the tower of the RNLI headquarters became visible. Home! I was going to make it!

The river was surging stronger than ever before as it neared the ocean, threatening to take me past the exit and straight out to sea. I swam diagonally, and managed to reach the ramp without being swept away. As I tried to stand upright, I felt my blood and organs lurch inside of me. After being cradled for so long in the moving water, the sensation of being tipped to standing felt more wrong than right, and I staggered, scrabbling for a sense of balance.

D was waving to me from the riverbank. I hugged him, drenching him with river water, and he took a photograph of me. I was giddy with the thrill of having braved the unfamiliar and swum for longer than I had ever dared believe I could. It was impossible to push back the tide, it was impossible to predict the weather, but I had learned anew that it is ever possible to defy our expectations of ourselves – even if, as D gently reminded me as we feasted on fish and chips an hour later, those who love you believed you could do it all along. A lesson I was going to have to cling to over the coming months.

CHAPTER SEVEN
To Ithaca

Finally able to swim in open water, beyond the pool or my home beach, I let myself believe I was up to taking on a challenge I had been dreaming of for over a year, and had found tantalising for much longer: I wanted to swim in the Greek waters of the Ionian Sea. Specifically, I wanted to swim to Ithaca, the island home of Greek hero Odysseus.

Since childhood, I had been fascinated by Greek myths and the heroic tales of the Trojan War. The stories provided the sort of nerdy, hearty adventure that I loved hearing about, while the flamboyant, emotional antics on Mount Olympus fanned the flames of my increasingly passionate understanding of the world. Goddesses taking petty, brutal vengeance after suffering a broken heart; burly men dragging each other around in the dust in a decade-long war started by a pretty face – these were the issues my 1990s self dreamed of day and night. As I grew older and read classics at university, it became Odysseus who captured my imagination more than any other. By now, it wasn't just his war heroics that mesmerised me, but his ten-year voyage home from Troy to Greece.

Legend has it that Odysseus was within sight of Ithaca when the bag that Aeolus, the god of wind, had given him was opened while he slept by his over-curious crew. All hell – and indeed, all winds – was unleashed, and the ensuing storm meant that the ship and crew were blown hundreds of miles off course. It took several years to get home after that, not helped by Odysseus being held captive by the amorous Calypso for seven years. Yup, seven years he was stuck on that island with the nymph, who was desperate to have him as her mortal husband. Meanwhile, his actual wife Penelope stayed at home on Ithaca, busily spending every night unpicking the embroidery she had completed during the day, having promised her suitors that she would marry one of them just as soon as her sewing was finished. Eventually, a full decade after Odysseus set out from Troy to return home, they were reunited. Sometimes you have to wait for the one you love.

It had been nearly twenty years that stories of his voyage had been stirring a yearning in me for a place to call home. Until the previous summer, I had not had anywhere that I really felt was home. My mother had grown up in the West Indies, to parents from France and Colombia, my father in Cornwall, but my father's work in the military meant that we had moved house every couple of years throughout my childhood. When I finished studying, my decision to live in London was based on convenience and the heady glamour of Britpop rather than any sense of wanting to make it my home. Home had only ever been where the ones I loved were.

Now, Brighton was home, and our flat – despite the soggy aftermath of the flood of the previous summer – was the first place I had ever felt as an adult that I truly belonged. This was less to do with my surrendering to the idea that falling in love and getting married made everything okay, and more because I had been on my own odyssey for the best part of a decade before that. I never wanted to be Penelope; instead, I had fought for years to be my own hero, my own Odysseus. I wanted my sense of belonging to come from within, and as soon as I found that, I found D. Now that I had my own Ithaca, I wanted to see the real one – and I wanted to do it across the sea.

Unfortunately, my husband had not been entirely privy to my inner quest, and merely thought I wanted to go on holiday.

'But it's HEROIC,' I said, leaning sassily against the kitchen table, with my swimming towel draped across me in a manner that I liked to think brought to mind a Grecian youth. He agreed quietly and started to unload the washing machine.

My trip may well have been heroic to me, but my husband's job is also frustratingly noble stuff, employed as he is in equalities work in Brighton. Consequently, there ensued some tense marital negotiations: his busy summer schedule, working on both Pride and Trans Pride, the dates available to take the trip, and the amount of time I would need to ready myself to swim five kilometres per day were all taken into consideration.

There was one extra deadline we were contending with: after a year of marriage and even longer of trying for a baby, we had recently been referred for IVF treatment. My family is almost indecently prolific with its offspring – my mother is one of five siblings, all of whom have three or more children. My first cousin even has two sets of twins.

The idea of having to navigate fertility treatment was not one that I had seriously considered. But that spring, after a series of tests for both us, we were told that if we wanted children, IVF was the route we must take. I was shaken by the news. My relationship with my body had changed radically over the last few years. Finally learning to have a little faith in what it was capable of had been one of the most rewarding experiences of my life. Now, I was being told that positive thinking and a sensible training plan was not going to be enough.

The afternoon we were given the news, I sincerely felt that I had been robbed of a future life experience. An essential connection was not working between us. The thing we had both wanted for so long was so much further from our reach than we had ever imagined.

That evening, I sat and watched, softly sobbing, as a pale April sea lapped gently against the pebbles. Whether it's sweat, tears or seawater, salt water cures everything, my grandmother had told me. Well it couldn't cure this. I wondered what ever could.

The fug of sadness lifted somewhat once we had been to some initial consultations and had the procedure explained to us. I would take the contraceptive pill for a month to stop my menstrual cycle. Then I would have weeks of self-administered injections to act on my pituitary gland, stopping the production of natural hormones to control the release of eggs from my ovaries, followed by two or three weeks of further treatment to stimulate my ovaries into creating more than the average one egg per month. Finally, after several scans a week to monitor their progress, I would take one final, precisely timed shot to make me ovulate, before having an operation – under full sedation – to remove the eggs I had created. In the lab next door to where I was lying unconscious, these would be introduced to my husband's sperm, and if we were lucky enough to create any embryos, one would be put back into my uterus a few days later. The combination of drugs, scans and significantly more invasive medical procedures than I had ever anticipated meant that there was no way I could take a swimming holiday in the middle of the treatment, which was the only time D could go away.

Thus, the decision was made: I would go to Greece alone, before treatment began. Much as I longed to take the trip with my husband, circumstances meant I really did have to be my own Odysseus this time.

Six weeks later, I was on my way to the island of Lefkada, where I was going to spend a week in a small family-run hotel as part of a guided swimming trip around the islands of the Ionian. It would be a final chance to experience that sense of flow, the relaxation, the rhythm of nature, restoring my faith in what my body could do, regardless of the limitations it was putting on me. It would be an opportunity to see what I was capable of in the water, and to remind myself of the barriers I had overcome, even as I was now confronting a new one.

I spent the weeks before the trip researching Greek politics. The financial crisis that summer meant that by the time I was on my way to Gatwick, the country seemed to be on a knife edge. The Foreign Office was advising travellers to the country to take all the money we would need in cash only, as automated bank machines were no longer permitting non-nationals to use them, and queues inside banks were enormous. News broadcasts were also encouraging tourists to spend whatever we could in local shops and tavernas in order to pump money back into the economy. The thought of travelling alone seemed more daunting than it had done for years. The sooner I got to Greece and began to distract myself with my aquatic challenge, the better.

The evening I arrived was heavy with heat and the Mediterranean holiday hum of fans and cicadas. In the distance, a kitchen radio was babbling away as we all gathered on a terrace overlooking the sea to introduce ourselves and eat together under the vines. J, the leader of the trip, encouraged us to go around the table saying a little about ourselves and our swimming experience. This was the moment when I realised just how enormous my capacity for over-optimism could be.

'Hi, my name is Jess and I recently swam the English Channel as part of a relay with some mates.'

'Hi, my name is Michael. I came on this trip last year and take at least one swim trip abroad each year.'

'Hi, my wife and I are regular Masters swimmers in the South of France; these are our times . . .'

'Hi, I'm on this trip with my teenage daughter as a rest before her Olympic tryouts.'

And so it went, on and on. These were people who had swum *for* their country, who had swum *across* their country and who had swum *to* their country. Yes, they all seemed very friendly. But they may as well have been a different species. It was certainly going to be an interesting week, even if it turned into one that cost me the use of my arms.

The first morning, after a quick breakfast, we met in the bay by the guest house and boarded a beautiful wooden boat named *Mowgli*. It had a cabin, a shady canopy at the back, a generous deck at the front and a taciturn Greek captain who made no effort to hide the fact that he despaired of all of us and our sanity.

The pattern for the week was quickly set. We would get on board with what we'd need for the day – little more than suncream, hats, goggles and flip-flops – and as the boat headed out to wherever the swim was to begin, we would be briefed on deck about what type of swim it would be. Some were coastal, all the way around an island, with plenty to look at below us; some would be crossings from island to island – more satisfying, but potentially much harder work. And some would be a combination of the two. For most of the week we would have a morning swim, lunch somewhere nearby, then a bit of time on the boat before a second swim. Friday would be the exception, as that was the day of the heroic five-kilometre swim from Kefalonia to Ithaca.

En route to our first swim, we were talked through the various safety measures that were non-negotiable on the trip: we had to wear goggles and suncream, and we would all have the seams of our swimsuits Vaselined up for us. We weren't to do it ourselves, as that would inevitably lead to hideously smeared goggles. Instead, one of the trip leaders would do it, wearing a pair of surgical latex gloves. After that, we would enter the water in three separate groups, divided according to ability and denoted by different-coloured caps. Each group would be followed by a small rubber rescue dinghy, driven by one of the instructors, containing bottles of water, mouthwash, some food and a first aid kit. Freedom, and safety.

First we had to be divided into our groups, so the boat's initial stop was at a small bay, where we were asked to get in and swim for about three or four hundred metres, watched by

J. I hadn't warmed up, or even been in the water yet. I was nervous, flustered, but determined not to let myself down by panicking like I had done in the past.

Clambering cautiously down the boat's ladder that first time, the water was cool against my hot skin but still felt like a warm cup of tea in comparison to Brighton's on-the-rocks chilliness. It was thick with salt, which, on initial entry, gave the sea an almost trampoline-like amount of bounce. But once my face was in, I experienced the other side to the salt, which quickly coated the inner rim of my lips as I exhaled, slack-lipped, into the blue. I closed my eyes, kept myself calm, concentrated on my stroke and swam the distance. Then I headed back to the boat, where I was immediately assigned to the bottom group.

That decided, we took it in turns to swim towards and then past one of the instructors, who was filming us underwater so that later in the day our strokes could be analysed by the group. It was an enlightening afternoon, sitting at a bayside taverna in front of a large TV, watching all of the different ways there are to do the same thing. Among us there were swimmers whose legs barely moved, whose legs kicked in near frenzy, whose arms swung out wide or whose arms barely seemed to bend at all. As with running, I was realising that everybody is different; each of us carries a lifetime of scars, sprains and surprises. No kink was the same, no movement comparable. Seen individually, there were those who looked as if they would barely get through the water at all, though when I watched them in the group, I could tell that they were comfortably beating some of the others. Likewise, my stroke was okay, but my strength and experience much less than the rest of the swimmers.

That first day's swimming was not too taxing, but being in

an entirely unfamiliar environment was all-consuming. I was used to wading into the water; a slow walk with a gradual drop-off. Now we were clambering or jumping off a boat, straight into deep water. The most striking thing was its clarity. I had never seen anything like it. In Brighton there are only a few days when the water is clear enough to see through, and even more rarely is the ocean floor visible. Now, I could see a whole new universe of sea life, from coral to creatures.

I had always known I was swimming among fish in Brighton – the occasional rows of fishermen along the shore were a bit of a giveaway. I once cheerily asked if they ever caught anything, only for one of them to hold his hands two feet apart to demonstrate the size of a mackerel. Now I could actually see the fish beneath me. A sea urchin here, a slippery silver fish there, and countless starfish on the rocky sides of the islands. The fabric of the ocean floor itself was like nothing I'd seen, with its monochrome rock and sandy bottom beneath, far too deep to reach.

Then, as I breathed, I would look up and see nothing but blue skies, and charcoal-grey rock with endless rugged trees scattered across it. It felt like tasting dense, fibrous meat after six years running and swimming alongside the saccharine-sweet Regency facades of Brighton and Hove, and within twenty-four hours I was happily adapted to the rhythm of the trip. None of the individual swims were too taxing, and we had plenty of rest and food between them, so I let the watery world become my world. We glided into caves, feeling like explorers or battle-worn Ancient Greeks seeking shelter on the way home. We bobbed in water choppy from passing oligarchs' yachts. And we swam in still early-morning seas that were as cool and calm as a Scottish dew pond.

There was, however, one thing holding me back. Surprisingly, it was not my swimming ability; rather that the water getting into my eyes was forcing me to stop and adjust my goggles. Since my first lessons in the pool, fiddling with my goggles had been something of a nervous tic, a way of playing for time while I caught my breath and my bearings. Now, it was becoming a frequent necessity. The salt water was savage, the light was brutal, and the combination of the two was almost unbearable. The salt felt rough, as if each individual ragged sodium crystal were rubbing against either my eyes or my lips. The Vaseline around my seams, which had seemed wildly overcautious two days ago, now made perfect sense. If only I could apply something similar to my eyeballs.

Since the previous summer, I had been using a large pair of goggles. I hated the sensation of the rubber seal pressing into my eye sockets, so had selected a pair that were almost like a snorkelling mask. I had ordered a new, tighter pair for the trip. But with both pairs, a few drops of water would sneak in before long. Until now, that had been how long I would swim for at any one go without treading water to orientate myself. With these new swimming companions, and in this environment, this was far from good enough. Even the slowest group was happily swimming at a steady pace for twenty minutes at a continuous stretch. I simply couldn't do it.

How was no one else suffering from the salt water? It was only taking about ten strokes before, each time I turned my head to breathe, that first drop was dripping from the centre of the goggles and down onto my opened eyeball. Like lemon juice on a fresh paper cut, it was a sharp sting each and every time. It didn't matter if I tried to keep my eyes closed; the water would just pool at the edges of the goggles, becoming abrasive against the seal and bathing the soft skin around my eyes in what felt like acid.

When we stopped for lunch on the second day, in 39° heat, my eyes were streaming as if I had suffered a horrible allergic reaction. My whole face had blown up, swollen and red. Families on other tables were pointing at me as if I were some sort of cautionary tale about the dangers of terrible sunburn, or head-butting wasps. The shame was a speck of dust, though, in comparison to the pain that every single blink brought about. I walked round to the back of the taverna and poured nearly an entire bottle of fresh mineral water into my eyes. It helped, but it didn't solve the problem.

As *Mowgli* set sail the next morning, I started to fret about the pain the salt would surely bring me again today. But the group was a cheery one, and I had begun to feel confident about asking questions of everyone – whether about their lives, their passions or their swimming kit. There was a mum who left her kids with her husband for a week every year to come on a trip like this, two pairs of mothers and daughters swimming together, and a myriad other intricate and personal journeys that had brought us all to this boat. There were quiet, mild-mannered teachers who had swum the Channel, alpha-male businessmen who had little sea-swimming experience but boundless determination, and those who simply loved the sea and spent all year swimming in pools, saving for a trip like this one. There was also a world of kit and devices, from mono fins that let you swim like a mermaid to handy waterproof bags that I had never encountered before. Surely someone on the boat would have something to help my eyes. I asked around about

what everyone else was doing to overcome the pain of the salt
water.

'Is there some sort of wonderful spray I can use to wash my
eyes out every half-hour or so?' I casually asked.

'What do you mean?' replied one of the others.

'To wash out the salt water. I can't handle it any more, it's
stopping me from swimming properly.' I put a little extra effort
into sounding relaxed, as four pairs of eyes, including one of
the instructors, were now facing my way.

'Water shouldn't be getting in your eyes if you're wearing
goggles.'

'Well, a little bit always gets in after a few minutes, doesn't
it?' A cheery smile. 'Then you have to rinse and adjust!'

'No. You don't. If your goggles fit, you should never, ever
take them off in the water. Your eyes should be entirely dry for
the whole swim.'

Now this was news. Big news.

'But isn't getting water in your eyes just one of those things,
like maybe a blister on a rainy run in new trainers?'

'No. It really isn't. This is such salty water. You can't swim
properly if you keep getting it in your eyes.'

'Well, this I know. I just thought I had to . . . deal with it.'

Giggles started to break out among the group on the boat, as
the rest of them gathered round.

'So when you're swimming, you have water in your eyes
from the first few minutes?'

'Yes. Why do you think I keep stopping?'

And with that the penny dropped. Soon people were rooting
around in their bags, passing me spare goggles and helping me
to put them on. It hadn't passed me by that many of them were

wearing the same brand, and most of them had extras. People were thrusting multiple goggles on me, encouraging me to try on different pairs.

'Why are you shoving them into your eye sockets like that?'

'So they don't leak.'

'They don't need to be pressed so hard. Aren't you smearing the lens?'

'Yes, all the time. And my eyelashes touch the other side, which leaves smears too.'

'My God! How have you managed to swim at all?'

Turns out I had been squeezing my goggles to my face, trying to create some sort of suction, and in doing so I'd been breaking the seal, rendering them all but useless. My nervous tic of pressing them to check the tightness was undoing any tightness there was, and the goggles I owned did not fit the shape of my face at all. Within fifteen minutes, I had caused the first proper belly laugh of the trip for some of the group (you're welcome, guys) and also promised them that I would try wearing a different pair that afternoon in the water (thank you, Amy!).

That afternoon, I swam like I had never swum before. We were taking a crossing between the islands of Meganisi and Kithros, against currents of a strength hugely at odds with a sea that looked so flat and calm. Like a sly pupil passing notes under a school desk, the water's surface was a picture of beauty and innocence, while beneath it was moving, churning, agitating. But I could swim uninterrupted. Stroke after stroke I thrust my arms into the water, determined not to disappoint the group that had done so much to help me. I looked around beneath the surface to keep an eye on how well I was keeping up with them. My visibility was now so much clearer; I could see enough to even try and match their stroke rate. In our underwater world, body type had little effect on how we moved. The strength, the glide, the ease of the reach through the water was all that counted, and these more experienced swimmers, even in the lower group, had it all. The faster swimmers were easily taking the fewest strokes, and their faces looked the most relaxed. The breath, the extension, the mindset was everything.

And the mindset was challenging. I found the sensation of travelling between two bodies of land dizzyingly intimidating. Once, managing a single length of the pool had been too much for me. Then, swimming in open water, albeit close to the shore. Then, the unknown length and depth of the river. Each time, I had persuaded myself that if I could relax and focus, I could do it. Each time, I had been proved right. The barriers were not merely physical, but mental.

However, this was something else entirely. As we reached the furthest point between the islands, the sea became so deep, it turned colours I'd never seen before. It was beyond blue; a dark purple, almost charcoal, with shimmers of yellow as the current moved on and on below us. The sighting lessons we had repeatedly taken in Brighton, teaching us how to aim for landmarks on the skyline while allowing for the movement of the tides and current, now fell into place. We found ourselves righting and re-righting our course, having to fight to stay straight rather than being dragged somewhere else entirely. That pull in the water, begun as a ripple on the other side of the world, reached me then, in that moment, as if to gently tug my sleeve and let me know that perhaps, perhaps, I was reaching the limitations of what my body could do. And the thought stayed with me all week as we approached Friday, the day of the five-kilometre swim.

We had a pre-6 a.m. start that morning, to be ready for a boat trip of over two hours. I was tired, and beginning to ache in places I had never felt before. My lips were dry from the salt water, my arms were starting to feel tight, and my back and shoulders were sore but stretched, quite unlike they had ever felt after being hunched over a desk or lifting weights at the gym. A dull tiredness hummed though me, despite a succession of early nights. Few of us were drinking in the evenings, though I had nobly had the odd glass of wine before eating almost indecent amounts of food.

The mood on the boat was noticeably quieter than usual. Up until now, I had used the time spent in transit as valuable chatting time. I had enjoyed conversations with the group, getting tips on my technique as well as hearing stories of their entrancing swims around the world and what they had meant to them. There were those for whom swimming had provided solace in desperate times, those with frantic jobs who needed the mental and physical unravelling that it encouraged, and those for whom swimming five kilometres per day in the ocean was a spot of relaxation after years of Olympic training. Today's early start and the task ahead, though, had left us all but silent.

For me, this was agony. My nerves were mounting. Not only was it further than I had ever swum continuously – by over a kilometre – but we would be negotiating a busy channel, competing with swells and currents as well as holidaymakers' boats and billionaires' super-yachts. And there was the added pressure that we had been told to swim tightly in our groups during the crossing, directly alongside each other for safety: there was no option to slow down to catch my bearings, play with my goggles or indulge in panic. I would either let the team down or find myself drifting dangerously alone in the currents.

I sat in the prow of *Mowgli*, my legs dangling over the water as she moved slowly through the still, flat, unbroken surface, the sun rising behind the distant islands, and I felt terribly, horribly alone. I missed home with a longing I was sure only Odysseus had ever felt. For the others, this was an energetic holiday, but for me, it felt like a last chance to prove to myself what I was truly capable of before I faced the uncertainties of IVF.

Months earlier, when investigating other heroic swims, I had read about the young lovers, Leander and Hero, who had been separated by the Hellespont strait between Asia and Europe, meaning Leander had to swim towards his love every night. In Christopher Marlowe's famous poem, Leander would tie his robes on his head to make the crossing, utterly dependent on Hero lighting a lamp for him to sight as he swam to her. But the original Greek poem, by a now unknown poet named Musaeus, contained a line that truly struck a chord. He describes Leander, swimming alone:

To reach the lamp – voyaging in strange guise.
Himself the ship, mariner, and merchandise.

As I read those lines, they crystallised what was both so liberating and so terrifying about open-water swimming: when you're in the water, it's all down to you. You are boat, cargo and crew. That solitude, the space to let your eyeballs slacken and your mind, breath and being follow suit – that is the essence of why we swim. A sort of vertigo swept over me, rendering me dizzy with the possibilities.

As I stared down into the water, a dolphin's fin broke the surface and danced ahead of us. I yelped; the captain cut the engine. Emotion bubbled up in me as if I'd swallowed a lifetime of inspirational quotes and was struggling to keep them down. Sure, dolphins were lovely, I'd always thought, but I was far from being the sort of dreamer who felt that swimming with them would render my life better lived. In that instant, I saw I had been a fool. Not because the dolphins themselves were going to change the colour and texture of my life, but because only seconds before, I had been feeling so utterly alone, while mere metres from such a magnificent sight. The dolphin leapt and pranced ahead, before approaching the boat and swimming alongside it for a little while. I sobbed, overwhelmed at how appallingly close the lowest and the most beautiful moments can be to each other. Yes, we swim alone. But we can never truly know what swims alongside us.

Half an hour later, people started to ready themselves to head into the water. The tub of Vaseline was out, cotton clothing was coming off, and the volume of chatter began to rise. My heart was hammering.

It's all about the breath, I reminded myself. Keep the breath steady and you'll keep yourself steady.

Michael, one of my group, saw me standing on the edge of the boat, trying to take deep breaths. He was one of the swimmers I admired the most. A week ago we hadn't known each other, but we had since discovered that he had family in Trinidad who knew my grandparents, we had books we loved in common, and he had been nothing but gentle and patient with me and my attempts in the water all week. He had no athletic ambition for the trip, but that was presumably easy for him to say, as he had the most effortless stroke I had ever seen. He moved with such ease and grace that he seemed almost amphibian. I had never – and still haven't – seen anything as elegant in the water. Each stroke lasted an eternity. He dawdled, looked around, seemed to be putting minimal effort in yet getting maximum pleasure. A true inspiration.

He asked me if I was nervous, and we chatted about how much the swim meant to me: the challenge, the years of dreaming of Ithaca, and what might possibly be a last chance to have my body be all mine, and within the sphere of my understanding. In only ten days' time, the regime of daily injections for the IVF would begin, and after that, possibly pregnancy. Much longed for of course, but it would change everything, representing a break from the body I had fought so hard to get to know, to master and to love.

'We never stop learning, though, we never stop seeking,' he said. 'It's like the Tennyson poem.'

I had studied 'Ulysses' twenty years ago and remembered it was largely concerned with a refusal to surrender, regardless of age or what life throws at us. I felt I didn't really have the emotional space right then to start discussing England's great Victorian poet laureate, no matter how fine a man he might have been. But I was wrong. Because as the boat slowly slowed at our spot, Michael recited the final lines of the poem to me:

> that which we are, we are;
> One equal temper of heroic hearts,

Made weak by time and fate, but strong in will
To strive, to seek, to find, and not to yield.

It was exactly what I needed. I would be my own Odysseus, no matter what I was presented with. Now it was time to swim.

As with the River Arun swim, I became lost in sensory overload within the first few minutes of the crossing. The water was so deep, and the light so sharp, despite it only being mid-morning. Rays of sun repeatedly pierced a deep navy-blue sea and bounced up off the bottom, creating the illusion that the ocean floor itself was floodlit with enormous beams. My borrowed goggles were tinted for precisely these conditions; even so, they were barely able to cope. The light seemed liquid, leaping up and circling me every time I drew my hand through the water, trying to push against the current that was moving with such strength beneath me.

The group had agreed that we would take a hydration stop every twenty minutes or so, to break up what was estimated to be two and a half hours of swimming. The boat following us had several sports bottles attached with string to the picnic box they were stored in. The guide threw them in to us as we trod water, kicking hard to keep afloat. We sipped giddily and took huge swigs of the mouthwash we were also offered to try and counteract the taste of the salt in our mouths.

The first hour or so went smoothly, the group moving steadily as one, our breath and stroke keeping, what we now called our little pod, tight, safe amidst the channel. About halfway, something changed. We were approaching a small island to our left. It was a tiny island, barely big enough to lay a picnic blanket on, and until this point, we had been using it as a sighting point, keeping it in view in order to steer a straight course. We were to swim north of it as we passed, which we were all on course to do. As we approached, the ocean floor came up and back within sight. I couldn't really tell how deep it was, but I knew it was far too deep for me to reach. Still, there was some comfort in seeing the sloping patterns of the underside of the island beneath us. Until I realised it wasn't moving.

We were swimming at our hardest. Perfectly in rhythm, well warmed up, pulling hard, breathing hard. At last, I felt like a real swimmer. Except . . . I was going absolutely nowhere. An anxiety dream come to life. I was pulling and pushing at the water with all my might, but we had hit the point where the currents were at their strongest, and were amplified as gushing eddies coming round the tiny island. The harder I swam, the less I moved. The rocks below me were entirely static.

I continued like this for five or ten minutes before panic set in. I knew that to stop was to instantly slide back, away from the group. Exhale. Keep going. Exhale. Believe. Exhale. Glide. I glanced to my right, and saw that even Michael was having to work slightly harder.

But the demons were chasing me now. I had never stood toe to toe against nature in this way before. You can't fight nature, I thought, and as I did, I felt tears choke in my throat. I forced an exhale, thinking of my vagus nerve relaxing. I wouldn't let myself think it, I wouldn't. But I did. *If you can't fight nature, what about pregnancy?* I had thought it. And with that, I was lost in a world of worry. Would I ever get pregnant? What would IVF do to me? What would IVF do to *us*? Would it be worth it? Should we be trying to build our home for two into one for three if the signs all indicated that we couldn't? Would we get there? When would I know?

The water swirled around me and roared in my ears. I forced the air out of my lungs, again and again. The salt water was crusting my mouth, and every breath felt like a punch as the sunlight hit my eyes.

Think of home, think of home, think of home. Be your own hero, be your own Odysseus, be ship, cargo and crew.

I repeated these things to myself again and again, forcing physical relaxation until mental solace came. I made myself feel the power in my limbs and lungs, and love it. I was strong. Your body might never be the same after this summer, I told myself. Enjoy what you have. Think of home. Soon you will be home. You will make it.

Eventually, I won the battle. And it was a battle. Every push, every pull, every breath. The rocks beneath me slid slowly out of sight. The deep blue returned. I have never, ever been so glad to be swimming so utterly out of my depth.

But the horror wasn't over. About half an hour later, a sort of fizziness began in the tips of my fingers. I had only felt it once or twice before, in the final few metres of running events. I knew it meant that I needed oxygen, and fuel. The unintended consequence of my frequent goggles-based stops over the course of the last few months was that I simply hadn't built up enough endurance to keep going without these mini breaks. I realised what was happening and tried to power my way through with positive thinking. Success was limited. My mind had got me thus far, but my lungs had not had the chance to catch up.

My arms started to feel heavy in the water, slapping down

on the surface instead of cutting in and reaching forward. The swirling in front of my eyes seemed to be about more than the water churning around me. I stopped. I looked up. I needed help. I called to the rescue boat, and clung to it. J told the others to carry on, while I hauled myself into the boat. My breathing was laboured and erratic, my head spinning and the tips of my feet and fingers numb.

I breathed. I gulped at the orange juice on board to get some sugar into my system. I grabbed a handful of nuts. Devastated not to be in the water, I sat, breathing, for five minutes. We were so close to Ithaca. I could make out individual trees on the mountainside. Ten minutes later, I knew I couldn't let the dream go.

'Can I get back in?' I asked.

J checked me, to make sure I wasn't still delirious.

'I have to reach Ithaca. It's why I came.'

She nodded. I leapt off the boat – more the result of skidding on its rubber side than anything else – and headed for the grey rock. I couldn't believe there was any strength left in me, and I vowed never to forget the moment that the island's sea life started to make itself apparent to me. Once again the sea shallowed, and the ecosystems down there became visible. Fish shimmied between crags, sea urchins perched on ridges, and starfish danced on the side of the island. Red, yellow and orange, they had stuck themselves wherever there were gaps available, creating the appearance of arms in motion, waving at us. The starfish of Ithaca were voguing us home.

Finally I touched the rock, and burst into tears. Huge sobs, shaking my shoulders, forcing me to cling on to the island to keep myself steady. The others were already there, laughing and chatting. I had done it. I had discovered a grit I hadn't known I had, as well as a flexibility and adaptability that I had never imagined lay within me. Determination, potentially misplaced confidence and a basic understanding of training plans and fitness – these I had long had. But now, I had slowly, over a year of marriage and a year spent in the water, learned that strength does not always mean merely ploughing forward in the face of adversity; it means changing your plans when what you're doing isn't getting you where you need to go; it means allowing for your surroundings, for those around you and what they require, and it means nurturing the confidence to adapt without panicking.

The promise of home had set me free to explore, and the relaxation that swimming demanded of me had taught me that calmness is strength. As I clung to that rock, smiling down at those sassy starfish, I had no idea of the extent to which my adaptability and survival skills were about to be tested.

CHAPTER EIGHT

Winter

As the plane landed back on English soil, I smiled, knowing I would be home soon, and that there were still a few months before the most difficult stages of the IVF swung into action. I was gleeful to be returning to my Penelope, but it was tinged with the melancholy of knowing this summer was past full bloom. I wanted to carry on swimming outdoors, putting my new-found strength and confidence into practice.

I sincerely believed that I would be pregnant not long after my return from Greece. I was anxious about the side effects of doing a cycle of IVF, but I was not anxious about it failing.

I was wrong. It proved to be a brutal and disorientating experience that coincided with a bout of norovirus, involved an unexpectedly strong reaction to the stimulating drugs, and culminated in over a fortnight in bed. For days I was barely able to move because of the distended belly I grew when my ovaries created sixteen eggs within a fortnight; then, just days before the egg collection surgery took place, I was felled by the virus. The surgery took over twice as long as it was scheduled to, and when I came to, I felt as if someone with metal fingernails was scraping them through my uterus. We created one usable embryo, but the cycle ended in early September with me battle-scarred, exhausted far beyond running, and with a streak of red blood that confirmed the one thing I had barely had a chance to worry about: I was not pregnant.

The Saturday morning after we realised the treatment had not been successful brought a pale grey sky with rare glimmers of sunlight. I woke up at 6 a.m. and stared at the ceiling as the tears rolled slowly, silently down the sides of my face and onto the pillow. What now? Well, it turned out there was a chink of light in the autumn clouds: swimming.

I was by now part of a Facebook group set up for those who had finished the Pool to Pier course and were looking to swim in the sea, but not alone or as part of any formal training group. When I looked at my phone that morning and saw that others were planning to take a swim from Hove to Brighton, I knew that there was only one place I wanted to be. Only one place that would still my body and mind. I rolled over and whispered to my husband that I was heading out, to walk the two kilometres to the meeting point, and to swim home.

The summer had turned sour within days of my return from Greece, and I had only managed one sea swim before the IVF injections had taken hold. I had entered the sea on a sunny day, and left it only twenty minutes later, during a huge rainstorm, invigorated by the sonic curiosity of hearing rain hit the surface of the water when my head was below it. Since then, I hadn't been in the water for over a month.

As I walked down to the meeting point, the sun began to part the clouds, and before long there were three of us in the water, swimming east. Once again, I was experiencing the physical grit that sea swimming required of me, and the psychological solace it provided. It was a long swim, longer than I had ever done before along the seafront. But I was swimming homewards. When we reached the stretch of shoreline in front of my flat, I said goodbye to my swimming partners, and waved at D, who was standing waiting with a hug, tears and a towel. We sat looking out over the spot where he'd lost his wedding ring fifteen months before, and consoled each other over what else we had now lost. We couldn't tread water, we agreed; we had to keep moving.

Slowly, the overwhelming duvet of sadness that had swamped us began to shift. While the summer had not been the idyllic sea frenzy I had hoped for, once I looked up and beyond myself I saw that we were being treated to an exceptionally beautiful autumn. In fact, it barely felt like autumn. Day after day of endless blue skies seemed at last to suggest that absolutely anything was possible.

I can't imagine ever not feeling sad for that little embryo that didn't make it. That tiny cluster of cells that represented infinite possibilities. In addition to its actual loss, I had put aside countless plans for the autumn, anticipating physical changes that would have limited my usual predisposition to gallivant all over the country and beyond.

But after days of those wide-open skies and seemingly endless flat seas, I was reminded that I too was a bundle of cells with infinite potential. That we all are. Whereas for those first sad days it seemed like my life had been put on hold, now it began to feel as if a sliver of life had been handed back to me. We had agreed to try one more round of IVF, but for now I had a chink of time in which to use my body for as much adventure as it could manage. Sure, I was still a little swollen from the stimulation drugs, and lacking in fitness from the weeks I had been unable to run, but I was still here, wasn't I? It was time to make plans.

The first thing we decided to do was to visit D's dad and his girlfriend, who lived near the Lake District. I had never been there, but I had found myself increasingly tantalised by the idea of swimming in the area's seemingly endless beautiful waters. Having been brought up largely abroad, our family holidays had been mostly spent on the Continent – for us, driving to the Lakes would have been impossibly far-flung. Consequently, the area held a position in my mind not far from Narnia, or the kingdom of *Labyrinth*'s Jareth the Goblin King. This had been stoked by the fact that much of the talk on *Mowgli* had been of those who had either swum or were planning to swim Windermere or Coniston Water, the biggest of the two lakes, which regularly held large and increasingly popular organised swims of several miles. But beyond these few facts, I didn't really understand how many other places to swim there were up there, or how one might approach it if you weren't taking part in a formal event.

I had no interest in embarking on a proper training regime, and given that it was early autumn, it was the wrong time of year for entering outdoor swimming events anyway. But the minute the idea of taking a swim up in the Lake District had crossed my mind, a watery genie had been let out of its bottle. I spent hours searching the Outdoor Swimming Society's Facebook page for recommended swims and poring over pictures. I studied the body types of the swimmers in the images to see whether they looked dramatically hardier than me. Were these brave and noble types, I wondered, or just the ones with good cameras and patient partners with an eye for photography? I became borderline-addicted to putting the names of lakes and hills into Instagram and losing myself in the sliding walls of tiny square images. The more I looked, the less of a sense of perspective I seemed to have on what the Lake District was actually like.

When we got to my father-in-law's house, I spent a further couple of hours studying Ordnance Survey maps, Wainwright Walks maps, and Google Maps, before deciding that we could quite possibly spend every hour until Christmas researching. In the end, a Lake District research intervention was performed by D, and I went with what seemed like the simplest option. I chose to do what my father-in-law suggested: to simply walk up to a tarn where D as a child used to go with his family.

We woke early the next morning and set off for a drive that nearly gave me whiplash as my head flicked between my phone, where I was obsessively looking up definitions of geographical terms such as 'scree' and 'tarn', and the scenery that was unfolding ahead of me. I was under no illusion that the Lake District was anything other than mesmerisingly beautiful, but I was utterly unprepared for how much beauty, and how much variety it managed to pack into such a relatively small area. Just as I had finished craning my neck to see the picture-book prettiness of Windermere, so large that it seemed like the seaside rather than a single body of water, we were whizzing past huge, craggy, forested mountains, which reminded me of the regular drives my own family would take through the Alps when we lived in Germany during the 1980s.

The ever-changing views were all-encompassing, and D, who had holidayed there for years as a child, was entertained by my open-jawed amazement every time we turned a corner. 'It looks like something from *Star Wars*!' I yelped only a month or two before it was revealed that they actually had shot some of the new film there. But as the car slowed, and the dog – Tess, a whippet who had become my new greatest love – started to sense that we were nearly there, I felt my stomach lurch. What the hell was I doing? D hadn't seen me swim since June, when I had tackled the pier-to-pier swim surrounded by safety kayaks. And my father-in-law had never seen me get my toes wet in any way at all. I didn't know where we were going, and despite my endless googling, my confidence about getting in the water was based on posts I had seen online of others doing the same sort of thing. It wasn't like finally taking part in a 10K or a marathon, or even an event organised by my swimming course. There were no stewards, no lifeguards, no security rails – and no one to cancel the event if tide or temperature seemed too tough.

The Lake District is a series of fells (large hills) and peaks, covered in a variety of grass, forest, crag (black volcanic rock) and scree (smaller scrappy bits of rock that roll down, scattershot, from peaks, thus creating their own little snowy trails). Between them, either in the wide valleys between the mountains or in the gaps between multiple peaks, are bodies of water. Lower down, they are lakes – lush, populated and as pretty as a postcard. But higher up, nestling between the peaks, are the tarns – mountain lakes. Created by pooled rain or river water, they are usually smaller and significantly less verdant than the lakes. For someone who thought that the Lake District stopped at Beatrix Potter panoramas, their existence came as something of a surprise. They seemed . . . well, a little stark for someone like me. A little too hearty.

We left the car and headed up the fell, and I felt an impending sense of dread. Our walk was along a curving ridge around the side of the fell, in the shadow of Blencathra, the biggest mountain in the area. To our left was the edge of the lush green fell, sloping up and away from us. To the right was a perilous drop almost straight down to a distant outcrop of farm buildings, doll-like against the enormity of the backdrop, a river that seemed to be little more than a lick of nail varnish on a child's toy train set, and a smattering of sheep dotted around it as if arranged by the child itself. Tess gambolled on ahead, but because of the curve of the path she vanished almost immediately. From time to time she would pop back to see how we were, and well she might have wondered. Terror was starting to take an icy grip on me. We were just walking higher and higher, for nearly an hour, and I still couldn't see where I was going to be taking this most solitary of swims.

For someone who was used to being embraced by the watchful worlds of either formal learning or organised and insured sporting events, I was feeling increasingly alone. A world of what ifs was flooding my mind, as my breathing, laboured from the climb of the walk, started to stiffen with anxiety. Then, just as I had started to wonder if there actually was any water ahead, I saw the tarn.

It wasn't so much that it was a landscape unlike any I had ever seen before; it was more that it looked like the goddamn moon. Completely surrounded by rock and tumbling scree, it seemed as if the water was sitting perfectly in the top of a lunar crater. The slopes surrounding it were covered in scrubby grey, green and pale brown clumps of grass. Poking between the grass was black volcanic rock, as if someone had tipped the slate roofs of an entire town from the skies above and left them to shatter and smash. The edges of the water were black, littered with chipped rock and slate. It was as inhospitable as any landscape I'd ever seen.

What followed was a level of terror that I had only ever experienced cumulatively before. When training for a marathon, nervous about a speech or sweating over a longed-for date, I usually had the sort of creeping anxiety that nagged and tugged at me, letting me get on with things but always there, tapping at my nerves. Before my first few running events, this grew into bursts of panic when I confronted injury, or simply the fear of how long and unpredictable a marathon course could be. But this was different. This wasn't mere nerves; it was utter terror. Condensed and distilled until sticky and potent. It was the espresso of fear.

But there was something that kept me from pegging it down that mountain faster than even Tess could run. It was the fact that it wasn't just terror I was experiencing. It was longing, too. The water of that tarn was as black and still as a spill of ink on a laminated school book. If I'd been told that not a soul had ever touched it, I would have believed it without hesitation. I had no idea how deep it was, how cold it was, or if anything was living in it. But I wanted to get in. I longed to get in.

I couldn't speak for the existence of any wildlife in that water, but I could speak for me. I had survived the misery of the last few months. I had survived loss more painful than I had ever imagined. But I had survived. And I would survive the almost paralysing fear of this swim. I was here. I was fine. And as I had promised my husband on the day of our wedding, I didn't want to just watch life flow by; I wanted to leap in.

In the event, it was perhaps less of a leap than a slow, shaky wade. I left my rucksack on a grassy clump next to where D had chosen to sit. I stripped down to my swimsuit and found my hat and goggles, sparing a special moment's thank-you to my Greek swimming companions for the fact that I would actually be able to see where I was swimming today. I pulled on the neoprene socks I had bought for walking in and out of open water, and headed for the tarn's edge.

At first the cold didn't hit me. At first. Then suddenly electric shocks rocketed from my toes up to my gut as my body registered it, a beat behind. Beneath my feet was slate and pebble, and I realised that the water was so clear that the black rock beneath was much closer to the surface than it looked: the edges were very shallow. I waded in, first ankle deep, then knee, then thigh. With every step I took, I disturbed more of the water, sending ripples across the entire surface, reminding everyone and everything that I was there.

Once the water was above my waist, I looked back at D, then plunged my face beneath the surface, exhaling slowly. All I wanted to do was to breathe in, to gasp, to cling to air as if it were life. But now, at last, I knew how counterproductive that was, and how right it would ultimately feel if I forced myself to push as much air as I could out of my lungs. And lo, the magic happened. Where the terror had been gripping me, a level of calm crept in, and I could feel the longing to swim more sharply than I could feel the panic about what might happen. I looked up, turned and yelled, 'It's okay! It's going to be okay!' D's smile suggested that it hadn't occurred to him it wouldn't be.

I turned back to the water, did three more deep breaths, then pushed myself up and off the rocky floor, letting my legs rise until I was lying flat, looking down. I was swimming. For a while, the floor of the tarn still seemed very close. The heaps of slate and rock were smooth, polished by the endless water, and there were no weeds, reeds or greenery. I saw the lid of a Coca Cola bottle, and little else. I swam slowly, letting my breath find a pattern as I stayed relatively close to the water's edge. The cold started to seep into my ears, under my swim hat and beneath my suit. But I focused on my breath, in, out, in out, keeping the rhythm going.

I turned. It was time to swim across the tarn. I shouted out that that was what I was doing, and headed off again, watching the patterns made by the rock beneath me as my breath slowly dragged me into the steady state of calm I craved. Then, as suddenly as the tarn itself had appeared, its floor disappeared. Within three strokes, my view had gone from endless slate to . . . absolutely nothing. I could see not a thing, and I didn't even understand if it was a change in the quality of the water itself, or simply its depth.

The tightness reappeared around my chest in an instant. Was I in very deep water now? Deeper than any I had swum in before? Or was I in . . . black water? What was underneath me? What was going to happen next? I had no idea. I had no idea about any of it. There was only one thing I was sure of: panicking was not an option. I had learnt the hard way that to panic was to lose control of my breathing, and to lose control of my breathing was to lose control of my swimming. And I was in the middle of a lake where the only way home was of my own making. Ship, cargo and crew.

In the absence of any other options, I kept swimming. A pull to the left, a pull to the right, a breath; a pull to the right, a pull to the left, a breath. I closed my eyes. I opened my eyes.

The view was exactly the same either way. I swam. I breathed. I was. And as I crossed the tarn's centre, a memory trickled into my mind as slowly and surely as that cold had crept its way under my swim cap. Patrick's words on that first one-day swimming course. You don't – you can't – know for sure what is beneath you when you swim outdoors. But now I knew more than that: that you can never be sure of anything. Yet, as with swimming, you keep going, you keep breathing, and then, when you reach an edge, you have lived more fully than before.

I couldn't know, I would never know, why that embryo didn't stay with me. I didn't know if the IVF would work next time, or ever. But I was still me, I was still alive, and it was my job to grasp every gulp of life that was there for me. And as I pulled my arm back again, I saw the slate on the opposite side of the tarn. I had made it.

My head jerked out of the water and I waved back to D on the hillside. As I did so, I took a huge gulp of water. I've never tasted anything like it: the cleanest, clearest, richest water I'd ever had. I could taste the mineral-rich rock as if I were actually licking it. I could taste life. I was alive.

As autumn progressed, I swam and I swam, feeling the strength flowing gently back. I had been utterly unprepared for the havoc that the drugs and surgery would wreak on my body. The drugs themselves, and the strength of my reaction to them, had left me with extra rolls of flesh that seemed to have sprouted within a fortnight. The belly that appeared as I grew those eggs stayed, as did the soft pouches of flesh sitting on my hips – a sort of bum bag of extra me that left so many of my clothes either ill-fitting or uncomfortable. My boobs were uncontrollably enormous – the sort of thing that teenage girls or mothers-to-be so often take delight in. For me, they did not represent an exciting new life change, merely serving as a daily reminder of what I didn't have. As did the significant amount of internal pain that the egg collection surgery had left me in – which meant that running, and its associated jiggle, was utterly out of the question.

Swimming, though, I still had. Slowly I emerged from this body that bore no relationship to the one I had built for myself over the previous five years, and I took on more and more swims, enriched weekly by the sights, smells and sounds that each one brought me.

I swam again in the Lake District, this time with Tess panicking at the water's edge, unable to tell that my whoops were of delight not danger. Stroke after stroke I waded through my fear of the reeds and the mysteries that I felt sure must be lurking between them. I even kept my breathing steady and swam softly forward as I looked down and saw what I later discovered was a pike gliding smoothly below me.

Soon we had a second round of IVF scheduled. Until then, I became ever more grandiose in my attempts to console myself about past disappointment and to steel myself for future pain. As well as that incessant tug, the desire to be a parent, I still felt fiercely protective towards my own body. Ours was a relatively new love, one hard won over miles run and distance now swum. It had taken years to accept that yes, my body had value, but that value lay more in where it could take me, what it could show me, than in any perceived visual pleasure it could provide for others. I tried to approach this latest quest with the spirit of adventure that had sprung so late in me but proved such a source of joy.

I would strive, seek, find – and not yield to any suggestion that my life or my body were lesser if they didn't incorporate motherhood. No matter how much I longed for it, motherhood could not be the only goal: as with every panicked breath I had wasted when the ability to swim had been in me all along, I had to find the resources for happiness and contentment in my own skin, regardless of the outcome of the IVF.

I muttered Tennyson's words softly to myself again as I entered the sea alone at ten o'clock on an autumn night. It was the once-in-a-generation blood moon, under which I was determined to swim. The prospect of bathing in the inky dark of a night sea beneath the looming blood red of the lunar phenomenon was a goal I couldn't miss, even if none of the swimmers I had hoped to go with were available. A brief plunge would still inspire fresh fertility and possibilities, I told D, as I begged him to come down to the seafront for company.

A month later, I began the second round of IVF treatment. On the advice of my doctor, I was doing exactly as I would have done otherwise, until I felt I couldn't. In this instance, it meant swimming around the Palace Pier in the dark with the group of friends I had now made from regular autumn sea swims. I was by this time used to swimming around the pier in daylight, having done it a couple of times on early autumn mornings, seeing the rides and the wooden slatted walkways I had run down so many times from an entirely new perspective.

That Halloween, we met long after dark, when the tide was as far out as it had been that first time I finally let myself exhale and enjoy swimming four months earlier. We had glow sticks on our heads and in our tow floats, and we swam in the shadow of the pier, whooping and laughing. I watched the fairground lights pierce the water and dance beneath its surface, a thousand candy colours fizzing between my fingertips. The sea had a strange viscosity in the dark, and as we swam, being careful to avoid lobster pots, I called to mind those Greek dolphins and wondered who else I was sharing the water with. Children waved down at us, and D, watching from the pier, heard a dad tell his children they were being ridiculous to imagine they could see anyone in the water. 'Stop getting so spooked by everything,' he told them, as D quietly took photos. 'Those shrieks were coming from the rides; no one would swim in the dark!'

The moment we returned to shore was made all the more exciting when we realised we were far more frightening to both passers-by and those who'd seen us from the pier than any of the gangs in fancy dress were. I shimmered inside, exhausted, but with blood abuzz to have had swimming take me somewhere else I would not have dared to go if I were already pregnant.

Resolute about keeping my fitness up, I swam lengths twice a week in the pool and kept on swimming in the sea, even as the heat slowly started to ebb from it. There were sharp, sunny mornings when sparkles seemed to shoot from the water's surface, and days when the sea was as flat and inscrutable as the sky, but the weather held, and so did my ability to swim. The day before my second egg collection surgery, I swam in the mouth of Shoreham Harbour, feeling my muscles read the movement of the water and warm my blood from within against the autumn chill. I had rebuilt myself. I was ready.

This time the treatment went well, and a few weeks later

we had a positive pregnancy test. It was followed soon after by the heartbreak of miscarriage. The first round had been disappointment, a setback. This round was crushing grief. An ocean of tears for a life lost, and an almost total collapse in everything I had believed of my body. It had betrayed me.

Where I had found strength, I now saw inadequacy, insufficiency, weakness. Where I had found beauty, I now saw flesh that served no purpose: a nascent belly, swollen from medication but aching with emptiness, uncontainable breasts bursting with anything but sexuality. Where I had felt self-love, I now saw an unwelcome stranger in the mirror. That tiny, perfect red pearl of cells in my knickers: my body had been rejected, and in turn I rejected my body.

CHAPTER NINE
And to Spring

It takes a very long time for the ocean's temperature to change. As winter draws in, the water holds the heat of the rays the sun shone on it weeks previously. As the spring sun warms the earth, bringing trees to blossom, the sea stays stubbornly cold, remembering the short winter days. As Christmas approached, I felt the same, stuck in the sunless sadness of six weeks ago. Wave after wave of post-pregnancy hormones and IVF drugs ran through me; I felt as if I were fighting currents stronger than any I had ever had to navigate.

The first time I felt strong enough to get back into the water was a celebration. It was December, and Fiona, a friend from my swimming group, had reached the final mile of the fifty she had decided to swim to celebrate her fiftieth birthday, as well as to raise money for Amaze, the children's charity that had helped her and her son Dan for many years. We met beside the pier, a huge crowd of swimmers and onlookers, as well as the instructors who had taught me over a year before.

The sea was choppy; I wasn't sure what I could manage. But as I looked around, rubbing my hands together against the cold,

I knew that all of us could and would manage more than we ever imagined. Children were waving their mothers off, husbands were warming their wives up, swimmers were hugging and laughing. The celebratory mood buoyed me up as we leapt into the water, heading for the end of the pier.

The tide was going out by the time we came back in. It was a struggle to reach the shore. Each time I swam almost far enough to stand, the wash would suck me back. My head under the water, I heard the clatter of the pebbles dragging out into the sea, and wondered if I'd ever make that final stretch. After the last few weeks, it was a familiar feeling, but one I'd had on land more than at sea. I decided to fight. I would get home.

Ten minutes later, exhausted and trying to take off a swimming costume and eat a slice of cake at the same time, the idea that I had doubted myself seemed daft. The gathered throng was now even more celebratory than before the swim. There were people I had barely a thing in common with beyond a new-found passion for the water. There were people who had experienced things more gruelling, more painful than I could ever imagine. But above all there were people who knew that life can't be spent as a spectator; we have to get in and take part.

What followed that December swim was an experience I had never dreamed I would attempt: a full winter of cold-water swimming. I never chose to do it; I just chose not to stop doing it. Where so many other plans around me had turned to dust, in one area at least I just had to keep going.

Jumping into cold water if you are not accustomed to it can put huge pressure on your heart, send your breathing into potentially unrecoverable erratic fits and starts, and leave you woozy with hypothermia – too sleepy to swim, too cold to recover. You can't fight thermodynamics any more than you can fight infertility. But you can adapt. You can acclimatise. You can find joy where others see pain. And this was what I chose. To acclimatise. To keep swimming, week in, week out, until what had seemed like an impossibility, a madness, became golden, a delight.

Unlike with a marathon, a half or a triathlon, this challenge was never about a distance or a time. It was unmeasurable and unwitnessed by cheering crowds or sponsored cameras. There was no medal, and never would be. The challenge was simply to keep going. Slowly, daily, weekly, to keep adapting the threshold of what I was capable of.

Once a week, at least, I headed outside and took a swim. Usually it was in the sea. I met others, armed with woollens and flasks, and headed out towards the pier, the power station or simply a boat on the horizon, for as long as we could take it. Or I walked down to the seafront with D, who would sit, cradling a coffee, watching me, watching the sky. If I needed to be in London, I would find one of my beloved lidos, now learning which among them were unheated, shifting to cold water with the season's change. But it was enough simply to swim outside, catching snatches of the sky above me as I turned my head to breathe. A few days before Christmas, when I was feeling less than festive and needed to spur myself into believing that there were still smiles somewhere inside of me, I headed to Brockwell Lido, feeling the sub-10° temperatures sting my hands and feet as I entered beneath the sun's low early-morning light. I arrived shivering and timid. I left feeling like a warrior queen.

On New Year's Day, I swam with the group in Brighton: a loose collection of us arranged online, old faces and new. Most of us, including me, were in nothing but swimming costumes, shrieking and giggling as we dived in, passing families and dog-walkers not knowing whether to panic or cheer. I emerged puce into D's arms, skin and bones fizzing with cold – and the realisation that if I could cope with this, I could cope with anything the new year threw at us.

A couple of weeks later, I attended the PHISH (Parliament Hill Ice Swim Hootenanny) cold-water swimming event at the Parliament Hill Lido on Hampstead Heath. It was a bitterly cold day in early January; after a strangely warm Christmas, the first day of the winter to properly snatch your breath away. Nevertheless, from 9 a.m. until after dusk, men and women of all ages queued, raced, cheered and saunaed, while drinking positively Scandinavian quantities of coffee. The icy sub-6° temperatures didn't put anyone off, and there were almost more contestants than could be accommodated, all after the chance to race two, four or even more lengths in that water. The competitors themselves ranged from the aggressively competitive to those who had been swimming outdoors for a lifetime, feeling the cold invigorate them year in, year out, knowing that eventually the sun always returned. And the winners were spread across the two. For every back-slapping, high-intensity-training, expensive-kit-wearing thirty-something bloke, there was a solid, unintimidated matriarch more than able to cut through the pool just as fast, with perfectly even breath and significantly less fuss.

Through January, February and on towards March, the coldest month, I carried on swimming. Though the sea temperature dropped incrementally each week, my body, as it slowly acclimatised, felt the same each time. At first we would wade into the water, feeling the tiny prickles of cold work their way up our legs. There were smiles and yelps as we teased and encouraged each other. When we reached chest depth, the instinct for a sharp inhalation would seize us, the iron band of cold and doubt slowly tightening around our chests. So we would exhale, regulate our breath, remind ourselves that we could do this, that we chose to do this. Then the chatter would die down as we started to swim. The cold would grip my face – a firm, freezing hand squeezing at my jaw. I'd feel my hands stiffen in the icy water and make sure I kept them strong, elegant, reaching. The trickle of water made its glacial progress up my back, waiting to be warmed by the heat of my blood. I'd wonder how long I would last, if I would even make it beyond the waves to where the water was calmer. I'd breathe, I'd feel myself both start to move and reach a point of stillness.

I breathe, I push, I pull. I am.

After five minutes or so, my body would start to warm me from within, the hard work of the swimming pushing heat as far as it could out into my limbs. Usually, before returning to shore, I would flip onto my back, and take a bit of time to stare at the sky as I floated. I would feel the sun on my limbs, even as the cold water licked them from below. On our return, my skin would have turned a glowing red, as if I'd received a thousand tiny slaps – a sort of cold-water tan. I would feel the humming of my body working hard internally, organs buzzing with activity as they tried to keep me warm, to keep me steady as I dried myself, took off my swimming costume and got dressed on the beach with as much dignity as possible.

Sometimes I would be shaking, my teeth chattering, so I'd walk home fast, sipping coffee. Sometimes I was too cold to move for a few minutes, and would bend over, my fingers splayed behind me and my back to the sun, trying to make myself as wide as possible in order to catch the most rays. Within half an hour, I would be glowing from within, warm for the rest of the day. Like a hangover in reverse, I had done something that was painful for moments but that left me feeling well for hours. I had made the difficult habitual, the habitual easy, and the easy beautiful.

There is an increasing amount of research into the positive effects of cold-water immersion, in particular swimming, on the body and the mind. A German study has discovered that swimming in cold water reduces level of uric acid in the body, making us better able to cope with stress. Even simply sitting in cold water has been proven to decrease the heart rate by nearly 10 per cent – this lowers the blood pressure, creating a feeling of calm. And recent research has shown that cold water can have a positive effect on patients with depression or anxiety, decreasing cortisol levels.

For me, the winter of swimming was a sort of inadvertent exposure therapy. A type of behavioural therapy used to treat anxiety disorders, exposure therapy usually involves helping people to confront their fears by exposing them in tiny, almost insignificant amounts to the thing they are most afraid of, until they are so accustomed to it that it ceases to worry them.

Over the winter, I repeatedly exposed myself to the elements. With a series of small, recurring shocks as I hit the water day after day, I took myself to a place I never thought I could go, reminding myself just how much I could withstand as

I witnessed body and mind rise to the challenge of cold water again and again. Previously distressed at having reached the limits of what my body could do for me, I rediscovered pride in what it could achieve and where it could take me.

More importantly, I was exposing myself to myself. In a world where 'bikini bodies' are prized as the ones of most value, to feel happy in swimwear became not just a challenge but a source of comfort. That winter, I was the heaviest I had ever been. At the time, it felt like weakness, like surrender, but now I see that what felt like unnecessary blubber from hormones, grief or greed was helping me, keeping me warm, keeping me in the water to do what I needed to do. Moving, flowing, accepting. To thrive at the weight I was felt not just subversive, but a triumph.

I was emerging from the water calm but energised. After weeks when all that had coursed through me was the exhausting, erratic drumbeat of adrenaline and the insidious creep of cortisol, I felt as if I'd given myself fresh blood. Calmer, fitter, stronger. I could do more than I'd imagined, and the more I swam, the more I witnessed others experiencing this alongside me. In the summer, I tried not to look at bodies in the pool or at the beach: I didn't want to be a contributing factor to the anxieties of swimwear. But as the winter months slid by and the water was calmer, emptier, I saw more. As I glided along in the lido, trying to still my breathing before putting my face under the water, I saw women slowly easing themselves down the steps, scars the length of their thighs. I saw injured shoulders ahead of me, struggling to swing their arms around but finding fluidity and peace in the water. I saw women who arrived at the seafront jangling with panic or sadness leaving it serene an hour later.

These people, these quiet everyday gladiators battling the wet and the cold, showed me time and again that it wasn't just me who headed for the water in times of distress. Women miscarry every day, many of them in conditions unimaginable to my relatively ordinary experience. There are people all around us dealing with sickness, injury and upset, but they choose to keep moving instead of standing at the edge of life, peering in. The more you swim, the more you see the change in people before and after the water, the more you realise you are not alone.

Because the water is not just somewhere to enter events, beat times and reach mile markers. It lends itself less than running does to the big sponsored challenge. It's the exercise for those who thought they couldn't exercise any more, or for those who want the release of endorphins without the sucker punch of competition and impact. It's for the scarred, the sick and the sad. We know the healing potential of water, its kindness to bodies that feel ungainly on land. When Esther Williams, the screen goddess of the 1940s, was asked as she turned ninety whether she still swam, she replied: 'Of course. It's the only sport you can do from your first bath to your last without hurting yourself.'

To be a swimmer is to see things from a different perspective. Roger Deakin, in his much-beloved *Waterlog*, calls it a 'frog's eye view'; my perspective is not just a visual one but emotional as well. The year-round swimmer who is not necessarily training for an event is a different beast to those who speak of 'a life lived in sweat', 'feeling the burn'. We know there will be days when you simply can't swim in the sea, but we also know there are days when other things must be dropped because it's too beautiful not to.

As I was told that summer we got married, swimming is a sort of meditation. It slows you down and opens you up, just as marriage has done for me. I used to long for D to come and see me swimming, so that he could marvel at what I had mastered, but now I realise he never needed to see it: he never doubted that I could do it.

When I think about never having a child, a sort of breathlessness, almost a vertigo, comes over me. The same metal vice tightens around my ribcage, the one I felt as I entered the sea those first few times, as I became aware of the Greek currents tugging me, as I entered that black tarn. I don't know if we will ever have a child. I don't even know if we have it in us to try IVF again. I just don't know; just as I never know for sure what swims beneath me as I push myself through open water.

What swimming – and in particular swimming outdoors – has taught me is not just that there is capability in me that I did not credit myself with possessing; it has taught me about my adaptability. It is not enough for me to swim in pools and lidos alone, no matter how much I love the primary-coloured elegance of Bristol's changing huts or the silvery lining of Parliament Hill's freezing depths. I cannot just head up and down, swimming back into my own wake as it smashes against the four neat walls. The sea might be holding the memories of the sun six weeks ago, but as you swim in it, you leave your wake behind you, surging forward to whatever your future holds.

And it is not enough to simply train hard and swim hard. You must adjust how you move, refine how you approach the water and embrace your environment. In swimming, as in life, I found fortitude and resilience when I needed them most, but I also found the courage to amend my plans, to change depending on what the weather, the tide or my own body had in store for me. I have learned not to be frightened by this; that life is to be lived as a participant, not a spectator.

The most useful thing that anyone said to me about dealing with grief is that you never really get over it. When you have difficulties with fertility or staying pregnant, the whole experience is a process of accepting that grief might be coming, that it might be round the corner. But is that not the very nature of love? To fall in love is to expose yourself to infinite potential for rejection or pain, and to be a parent is to accept a lifelong commitment to the unexpected, the uncontrollable and the unknown. To love truly, to love deeply, is to know that you might lose it in a heartbeat. In the same way that you never know if the wind will change when you're half a mile from the shore, or the waves might smash you in the face just as you gasp to breathe, you never know if to love is going to be to experience pain. That is never a reason not to do it, not to try.

The morning that I swung my legs out of bed and felt my feet hit four inches of water instead of carpet was a stark example of how each of us has no idea what we're going to wake up to on any given day. You just never know if it's all going to be okay. But if we only ever thought that, we'd never leave the house! We have to get up, get out and get moving. We have to swing our legs out of bed every morning and seize what swimming has taught me: that not knowing can never mean not doing. We must take gulps of air when we have space, but we must never forget to exhale. We must stand on the shore, proud of the life our bodies offer us, and accept that we'll never truly know what lies beneath the surface any more than we'll know what lies ahead. And then we must leap in.

PART 2

CHAPTER TEN
A Brief History of Swimming

As a species, we have been swimming for ever. Unborn, we swim in the womb; as infants, we splash in the tub; and as adults we simply carry on associating water with pleasure and relaxation. It has always been thus: the very earliest evidence of civilisation indicates that swimming was part of being a human, at whatever age, whether for fitness, transport or pure pleasure.

The Cave of Swimmers, in the Libyan part of the Sahara Desert – as featured in Michael Ondaatje's *The English Patient* – has small swimming figures etched upon its walls, looking almost as if they're flying. It is understood that the figures are now ten thousand years old, drawn at a time when the Sahara was significantly more watery than it is today.

In both the Louvre and New York's Metropolitan Museum of Art, you can see small Egyptian cosmetic spoons in the shape of female swimmers holding dishes ahead of them. Dating back to 1300–1400 BC, they are delicate, ornate and charming little figures, made of wood or alabaster. The women are swimming on their front, elongated as well as elegant, and appear relaxed, at ease with themselves and content in their environment. The little dishes were designed to hold kohl or other make-up. The artefacts call to mind the recent Charlotte Tilbury range of make-up bags featuring iconic 1970s Norman Parkinson photographs of Jerry Hall in swimwear. Both are equally beautiful, one just an update of the other.

In Classical Greece, swimming took on a heroic role. Socrates was a fan (albeit in a slightly curmudgeonly way, merely trying to persuade others to like it); and then, of course, there was the Homeric hero Odysseus, who spent ten years on the Mediterranean trying to get home, including two entire days in the water itself after being caught in a huge storm when he enraged Poseidon, god of the sea.

It wasn't just mythical heroes enjoying or enduring their time in the water, though. Also in the Louvre is a vase dating back to 520 BC by one of the anonymous painters employed by the potter Andokides. It shows a group of Amazon women relaxing by, and in, the water. One is swimming with a couple of fish beneath her, one is about to dive in, and one is moisturising herself post-swim with oil from a small *aryballos*, a jar more often used by male athletes. There are even a couple of soft swimming caps in the image. It looks like a lovely afternoon spent at the water, and offers a rare glimpse in swimming history of women enjoying themselves.

Roman swimming meant Julius Caesar upping the macho ante once again, cut off from the rest of his troops and swimming for his life to escape an Egyptian revolt. His heroic swim took place when he was in his fifties, and is described by Plutarch, who tells how he had to carry his sword and cloak in his mouth, holding his papers aloft with one hand while he swam with the other. Hardly recreational, but it did the trick: he escaped. It did, however, set the template for swimming's place in history for the next few hundred years – largely as a skill to be called upon in battle: useful, but hardly delightful.

The mood started to shift in the 1500s. Sir Thomas Elyot makes a reference to 'swymmynge' in his 1531 guide for would-be English gentlemen, suggesting a rebrand was coming, but things really took off with Everard Digby's 1587 book *De Arte Natandi* (*On the Art of Swimming*). Digby was a bit of a maverick all round. His opinions and campaigns – ranging from papism to the briefly fashionable teachings of Ramism and general disrespect towards his masters and fellow scholars, as well as his habit of honking a horn and 'hallooing' all day – eventually got him 'sent down' from St John's College, Cambridge. But as far as swimming was concerned, he was deadly serious. Despondent at how it had been so long relegated to martial uses only, left to what he dramatically called 'the depths of ignorance and the dust of oblivion', he was on a mission to restore its reputation. He wanted to rescue swimming, to make it a sport and a joy – something beyond a mere means of escape from marauding enemies.

There are so many wonderful books inspired by swimming – more than I could ever have imagined when I first felt the seawater around me on my wedding day – but regardless of Digby's hallooing antics, *De Arte Natandi* is my favourite. This is not just because of its irrepressible enthusiasm and the way so many of its instructions are still pertinent today, but also because of its forty gorgeous woodcut illustrations. Digby really is the ultimate enthusiast. He longs for us to share his passion, and is brilliant at explaining it properly to his readers. He also seems to be an advocate of positive body image, judging by his little anecdote concerning a frog and a toad, the issue being who looks like they might swim the best, and who actually can. Clue: the toad, despite looking as though it might do better in the water, simply 'sinketh right down'. Thank you, Digby; this is a lesson for all of us who have stood nervously at the water's edge.

De Arte Natandi – which was originally published in Latin, before being translated into English eight years later, and then into French – was an ambitious project. In Digby's day, there were no swimming pools, lidos or seaside holidays. Swimming took place in the sea, lakes or rivers, and was largely done by boatmen and other workers. But by writing his book in Latin, he was aiming it directly at educated gentlemen: he really wanted to improve swimming's status across society.

The book begins (as do most swimming courses today) with a chapter on getting used to the water. He recommends only swimming in daylight and in sufficiently warm weather (May to August is specified). But, wisely, he cautions against jumping in if you're too hot, recommending that one takes a few minutes to cool down in the shade first. He suggests avoiding reedy, muddy areas, and water 'in which animals may have been washed'. He also advises against swimming in the rain because of its effect on both visibility and the quality of the water. 'The drops do trouble the superficies of the water, hurteth the body, disturbeth the eyes and lastly, draining from the banks into the river, bringeth also with it whatsoever dung, straw, leaves and filth do lie near.' He is also an early advocate of not swimming alone, suggesting that his reader finds a swimming pal 'taller and stronger than himself'.

The chapters that follow tackle the performance of a variety of strokes, including some quite fancy arrangements that seem to be early synchronised swimming. What is clear throughout is Digby's enormous degree of faith in his fellow man (women seem to be of little concern to him). He believes we are made for swimming as much as the fish themselves, telling his readers that 'a man may swim with his face upwards, downwards; on his right side, on his left side; stand, sit, lie, carry his clothes and other things safely, walking the bottom of the waters: which no fish nor other creature can do'.

The main stroke he advocates is similar to modern-day breaststroke, and he recommends learning with someone holding your chin up at first. He also has a suggestion for Tudor armbands made from pig intestines: 'take two bladders, blow them full of wind and fasten them so together he may have them to lie under his armholes, which will easily bear him up'. Ta-da!

He talks the reader gently through diving; side-stroke, where 'the upper hand roweth like an oar'; and doggy paddle, or 'to swim like a dog'; and explains turning in the water, describing the swimmer gaining momentum by rolling side to side like a ship at sea. He even advocates the benefits of treading water, accompanied by a little vertical chap in the woodcut illustrations.

But the most beautiful moment is when he reassures readers that if they get tired, they always have a secret weapon to fall back on: backstroke. This, he declares, is a gift that Mother Nature 'hath denied even to the watery inhabitants of the sea. No fish, no fowl, nor other creature whatsoever that hath any living or being, either in the depth of the sea or the superficies of the water, swimmeth upon his back, man only excepted.'

And he's right. When I first read that sentence, I felt time wobble, as if I could reach back through 450 years and sense exactly what Digby did in those intoxicating moments towards the end of a challenging swim, when you gently turn and gaze at the sky. After half an hour of hard push and pull in cold water, to turn as you reach a patch of water warmed by the sun and feel its rays hit your belly is one of the sweetest sensations swimming can afford. Digby knew it, and I know it, and we both want you, the reader, to be a part of it.

He has no concern for racing or speed, only for the buzz of exercise taken and the relaxation that swimming can provide. He is quite specific about making a slow, cautious entry to the water. But it isn't just daydreaming on one's back that he finds delight in: before the book ends, he pops in some tips on stretching (in case of 'cramp or any other infirmity') and on some elaborate water-dancing techniques: lying on one's back and raising one foot at a time out of the water. But please take note – this should not be confused with his advice on how to clip your toenails in the water, which is also included.

By being charming, determined and specific, *De Arte Natandi* did eventually achieve its goal. Interest in swimming was revived during the Renaissance period, particularly given the era's respect for classical culture and the countless water exploits of the Greeks and Romans.

In 1724, Benjamin Franklin visited the UK to spread the word about the sport, putting on demonstrations and lessons in the River Thames. At the startling age of eleven, he had even invented the swim fin, explaining years later, in 1773, that his prototypes resembled 'painter's pallets', and describing his use of them in helping his stroke: 'In swimming I pushed the edges of these forward, and I struck the water with their flat surfaces as I drew them back. I remember I swam faster by means of these pallets, but they fatigued my wrists.' He even tried them on his feet before realising that the ankle kick required for breaststroke made them useless.

For centuries, breaststroke had continued to be the stroke most swimmers are recorded as having used. It was how Lord Byron made his famous heroic crossing of the Hellespont in 1810; it was what the splendidly top-hatted gentlemen of the UK's oldest swimming club were using (in the sea I now call my own) when they founded Brighton Swimming Club; and it was how in 1875 Matthew Webb made the first Channel crossing from England to France. There is occasional mention of side-stroke, described by Robert Patrick Watson (nineteenth-century journalist and one of Webb's informal swimming coaches) as 'the most beautiful and graceful means of transit through the water'. Despite its loveliness, though, it never really gained widespread popularity.

Side-stroke's relative obscurity makes sense given the feats that were being accomplished with breaststroke. The latter seemed obvious, instinctive – you could both see and breathe – and there were all manner of inventions and contraptions being created to train the swimmer out of the water. Moreover, the great Victorian building programme of creating swimming baths up and down the UK catered for everyone who wanted to practise the sport.

Meanwhile, overseas discoveries began to reveal the ways that indigenous peoples further afield were swimming. By 1844, the US painter George Catlin was describing a new stroke that involved doing something previously unheard of with the arms. Catlin was an author, painter and traveller who specialised in the unexplored American West and its native American Indian people. He visited several indigenous tribes, including the Mandan, the Ojibwa and the Iowa, painting striking portraits of the leaders in their full regalia.

The portraits were widely acclaimed, with the poet Charles Baudelaire asserting that Catlin had 'brought back alive the proud and free characters of these chiefs, both their nobility and manliness'. It seems his observations of the Mandan in particular were not merely restricted to static portrait style, because in journals published in the 1840s, he described seeing them swimming: 'The Indian, instead of parting his hands simultaneously under the chin, and making the stroke outward . . . throws his body alternately upon the left and the right side, raising one arm entirely above the water and reaching as far forward as he can, to dip it, while his whole weight and force are spent upon the one passing under him, like a paddle propelling him along.'

Here we have the first seeds of front crawl being sown; later that year, Catlin took things to the next level. He had teamed up with a Canadian entrepreneur to bring a group of Ojibwa Indians to the UK on a sort of tour for audiences of enquiring urbanites. These were the days when curious Victorians thought little of staring at unfamiliar 'savages' as a semi-educational pastime, and the *Spectator*'s reviewer is both fascinated and appalled by the trip. The article of March 1844 describes the Indians being paraded all around London, particularly at Catlin's exhibition of portraits in Piccadilly's prestigious Egyptian Hall, and even performing a war dance for Queen Victoria herself (to the reviewer's utter horror).

What cemented the strange trip's place in the history books was an invitation to the visitors from the British Swimming Society to take part in a race, promising the fastest Indian a silver medal. So in April 1844, the Ojibwa Indians arrived on horseback at the High Holborn baths – which had been pre-heated to extra-warm temperatures for them on the advice of their doctor. The crowds were spellbound, not just by the sight of the stripped Indians swimming at speeds faster than they were used to, but also by the style in which they were doing it.

The *Times* of 10 April 1844 describes their stroke as 'totally un-European. They lash the water violently with their arms, like the sails of a windmill, and beat downwards with their feet, blowing with force, and fanning grotesque antics. They then dived from one end of the bath to the other with the rapidity of an arrow, and almost as straight tension of limb.' Mesmerising though it was, this revolutionary arm style was not taken up by Londoners with any great haste. The mixed reviews of the Ojibwa's visit seem to have left Victorian England dismissing the stroke as barbaric, and it wasn't for another thirty years that someone else had a go at doing the same thing.

That someone was John Arthur Trudgen. He was born in Poplar, London, in 1852, but lived in Argentina from the age of eleven on account of his father's job with an enterprising engineering company based on the Isle of Dogs. Trudgen grew up unselfconsciously swimming with native South American children, all of whom easily and comfortably used the overarm stroke that had so confused the folk of London twenty years earlier. When he returned to England, he worked on the stroke, refining it quietly.

Britain was now a nation in the grip of swimming fever, with swimming clubs and championships sprouting all over the country. Schools had been including sport as part of their curriculum, and competitive swimming was ingrained in the system. Out of term, the advent of 'leisure time' meant that workers and their families were taking seaside holidays and relaxing in outdoor pools in beautiful locations up and down Britain.

By 1873, Trudgen was ready to debut his new-fangled stroke in competition, and entered a championship at the Lambeth Baths. His performance caused a sensation, with the *Swimming Record* of the time noting that he 'swam with both arms entirely out of the water, an action peculiar to Indians. His time was very fast, particularly for one who appears to know but little of swimming.' By 1875, he was winning English championship races, despite still using breaststroke legs. But sadly for him, his achievements went unnoticed, as that same year, Matthew Webb completed the first Channel crossing. Distance had won out over style in the imaginations of the Victorians, and it was Webb who dominated the headlines. Despite the new stroke starting to quietly catch on, Trudgen was largely forgotten for many years, returning to work as a machinist back home on the Isle of Dogs before dying in 1902.

Also in 1902, the Australian Richmond 'Dick' Cavill entered and won a hundred-yard race using a new style that he claimed had been inspired by Solomon Islander Alick Wickham. By using Trudgen's Ojibwa/Argentinian-inspired arm stroke, and adding the 'Australian kick' – moving the leg from knee to ankle up and down in the water – front crawl was finally born. (For years it was referred to as 'Australian crawl', or 'American crawl', presumably depending on who was discussing it, before 'front crawl' was eventually settled on.)

I had been taking swimming lessons for six months before I discovered that front crawl had only been invented barely one hundred years previously. The ease and confidence with which everyone seemed to be doing it had always suggested to me that it was some sort of instinct that sporty people simply possessed, and that I was either mentally or physically lacking for not having a natural understanding of how it worked. I was very wrong. And I was very, very relieved when I discovered the truth: yes, we are born with an instinct to play, to move, to relax in the water, but no, we are not born with a perfect front-crawl style. It is as natural to us to swim front crawl as it is to ride a bicycle – i.e., not natural at all.

Sure, once you have mastered riding a bike, you simply can't understand what on earth the fuss was about, but until you have tried, fallen repeatedly and finally succeeded, it all seems unimaginably complicated. Front crawl is the watery equivalent of this process. It has evolved from a combination of hundreds of years of travel, curiosity, competitiveness and a desire to move as efficiently as possible, but it is not the work of mere instinct. And anyone who suggests otherwise, or that it should be a doddle to pick up, is a fool.

You will notice that this potted history of swimming has so far made little mention of women. This is not, I suspect, because no women were swimming until the twentieth century, but rather because women's stories are often written as sidebars to the main event. While the gents were heroically performing feats and inventing new strokes and contraptions, women were more usually seen as curiosities performing spectacles instead of the magnificent athletes they so often were – and they were often doing it while being held back by significant restrictions.

In 1875 – the same year that Webb completed that first Channel crossing and Trudgen won his first race with front crawl – Agnes Beckwith, the daughter of a swimming professor, swam the Thames from London Bridge to Greenwich in one hour and seven minutes. She was fourteen years old. Ten days later, fifteen-year-old Emily Parker swam from London Bridge to Blackwall. Beckwith in particular was a pioneer of women's swimming, taking on all sorts of feats throughout her career – from swimming twenty miles down the Thames to swimming for a hundred hours in six days and spending thirty hours straight treading water in a tank at the Royal Aquarium.

She wisely made the point that swimming wasn't just good for maintaining the figure, but was also beneficial for general health, explaining that, 'Many ladies, indeed, take the pastime up solely as a means of obtaining a presentable physique, for it improves the chest and arms wonderfully. But, besides making muscle, the sport promotes the circulation, and on this account it has been found excellent for the woman of bad complexion, as a concomitant giving also a healthy appetite.'

Nevertheless, she was expected to undertake her adventures in heavy Victorian bathing suits – even doing her water tank feat in black silk trimmed with crimson. Meanwhile, in the US, modesty laws around the same time decreed that women (and the children who were, of course, with them) wear heavy layered outfits, which were impossible to swim in and increased the risk of drowning. Even when a national programme to teach people to swim was introduced, as late as the 1920s beaches were being patrolled by police charged with maintaining public decorum. In 1921, the formidable-sounding 39-year-old author Louise Rosine was arrested in Atlantic City for having bare knees on display and taking a swing at the arresting officer. She declared to the *New York Times*, 'The city has no right to tell me how I shall wear my clothes. It is none of their darn business. I will go to jail first.'

And so it has been that for over a hundred years, women on both sides of the Atlantic have been using swimming not just as a means of hitting the record books (like Gertrude Erdele, who in 1926 became the first woman to cross the Channel, and Mariam Saleh Binladen, a dentist from Saudi Arabia, who in 2016 was the first woman to swim the 101-mile length of the River Thames), but as a way of declaring ownership over their own bodies, and indeed using them to make a political point.

In 1920, Charlotte Epstein founded the Women's Swimming Association in New York, going on to persuade the Amateur Athletic Union to allow women to compete, and coaching many women to glory in the Olympics. A significant part of her legacy was her organisation of 'suffrage swims', raising money for the suffragettes' fight for votes for women.

The same year that Louise Rosine was arrested in Atlantic City, British swimmer Lily Smith announced that she was training to make the crossing to France with a very explicit mission in mind: 'I am going to swim the Channel in order to demonstrate that woman is the physical equal of man. I am going to put a stop forever to this twaddle about the weaker sex. Yes, I am a firm believer in woman's suffrage.'

In 2016, Mariam Binladen said, 'I wanted to show that a young woman from Saudi Arabia can achieve a lifelong ambition, whilst at the same time raise awareness of bigger causes, particularly the plight of thousands of suffering Syrian orphan refugees. I also want to encourage more women from around the world to participate in sport and show them that anything is possible.'

Lily Smith may not have managed to complete her Channel swim, but her larger goal was accomplished at least in part. Today, open-water swims and marathon swims are not generally gender-segregated, and it is largely accepted that in this sport at least, men and women are equals. Indeed, some of today's distance swimming records are held by women rather than men.

Women fought for outfits that gave them the freedom to swim because the alternatives were literally killing them. They campaigned to have the right to move unencumbered in the water by layer after layer of stiff Victorian fabric; they faced arrest to be allowed to get their knees out and feel the water around their legs; they risked death to prove that they could swim as well as men could.

Today, when I stare at those Amazonian women dancing in the water on the side of that vase made nearly three thousand years ago, I think of the women who drowned in crinolines lest a Victorian gentleman be forced to witness the horror of the sight of a female ankle. But I also think of today's pressure to look 'acceptable' for swimming in public. Today women are no longer drowning in crinolines. Instead, surrounded by swimwear images designed with little thought given to the range of women who want to swim, there are women who go to bed hungry, who go to the bathroom to vomit after lunch, who go online for diet pills that kill them from the inside out . . . lest a modern gentleman be forced to witness the horror of the sight of a little excess flesh.

When you tug at your swimsuit, wondering if your bikini

body might pass muster, give a moment's thanks for the liberty we do have in the water today. Bear in mind the women who fought for the freedom of movement we have beneath the surface. Give a little thought to Louise Rosine and her night in jail. And remember what the record books now show: when we are free to wear what lets us be our best and do our best, regardless of whether we look our best, we *can* be the best.

CHAPTER ELEVEN
The Basics of Front Crawl

It would be optimistic, indeed impractical, to suggest that you can learn to swim from reading a book alone. Realistically, a handful of lessons would absolutely be the best course of action to take – whether you plan on learning to swim from scratch or want to get to grips with front crawl as a new discipline. You do not need to sign up for endless hours of tuition, but you do need to commit to a realistic amount of time spent practising in the pool. As with running, your body needs to warm up, so the first three panicky lengths will never be representative of what you're capable of if you can persuade yourself to stay in the water for thirty. So to help you enter the water those first few times feeling a little calmer, here's a brief run-down of the basics of front crawl and how it is generally taught,

The most important thing you need to remember is that there is no perfect swimming style: front crawl in particular is still a stroke in evolution. There are, however, some basic core truths that can make the whole process significantly easier. As we now know, front crawl is a relatively new stroke, and there will always be a guru coming round the corner ready to revolutionise as much as confuse. Added to that, there are also those who are not afraid to chip in with their own advice, based on how they were taught back in the 1950s or 1960s. Perhaps this is where my extraordinary conviction that my elbows should never bend came from.

There are currently two dominant schools of teaching: Swim Smooth and Total Immersion. The ASA, our national body in the UK, teaches what is largely a Swim Smooth-type methodology, but both Swim Smooth and Total Immersion have books, DVDs, online videos, courses and coaches all over the country and beyond.

Swim Smooth is an Australia-based organisation, founded by Paul Newsome, a UK-born triathlete turned swimming coach. Its coaching method is simple and pragmatic, committed to a philosophy of 'coaching the swimmer, not the stroke'. It divides swimmers into various types according to their natural physical attributes, such as height, strength, gender and natural buoyancy, also taking account of their emotional relationship with swimming, and then works within those criteria. For example, the 'Arnie' type is a competitive swimmer who sees swimming as little more than a 'necessary event for triathlon', and who will often hold their breath while swimming as they're approaching it as more of a sprint. Whereas a 'Bambino' is an anxious new swimmer whose goals are more focused on health, and who consequently has little feel for the stroke or rhythm in the water.

Basing a teaching approach on the idea that we all have different bodies, motivations, anxieties and histories strikes me as eminently sensible. This philosophy that there is no one perfect style works particularly for open water, where the biggest advantage you can have is adaptability and capacity for change according to circumstances. Having sat on the beach minding bags and watching my friends, or on the boat in Greece as the other swimmers fought strong currents and my eyes streamed with salt water, I have seen first hand how different we all look. I've seen swimmers who slip through the water like anchovies, and those who sturdily plough through it like tug boats. I have learned not to judge what anyone's relationship with the water might be. This open-minded approach to each and every swimmer's assets is Swim Smooth's greatest advantage.

Total Immersion is more comparable to the idea of barefoot running – it's a holistic, almost hippyish philosophy, focusing more on the experience than the outcome. Its founder, Terry Laughlin, is a charismatic US-based swimming coach, whose teaching method concentrates on moving through the water as efficiently as possible, focusing on balance and streamlining rather than a hardcore regime of fitness and strength training. His mantra is that 'every lap I swim feels blissful' (I told you it could border on the hippyish), and he refers to Total Immersion swimming as 'fishlike swimming'. These are fanciful ways of putting his actually entirely sensible philosophy to his students: he simply believes that if we can learn to position ourselves as well and efficiently as possible in the water, we won't have to expend as much energy on shoving it out of the way when we want to move through it. In short, if we can make ourselves as sleek, pointy and fish-shaped as possible, we will be able to focus on feeling graceful, beautiful and relaxed in the water, instead of churning, kicking and pulling our way through it.

For those first few weeks, you may curse him. Terry writes

about swimming with an extraordinary level of enthusiasm: think Everard Digby crossed with a four-year-old describing the Lego they were given for their birthday. However, his book does not approach the basics of front crawl in a particularly accessible way. There are no clear stages for the absolute beginner in the stroke. Instead, his chapters have titles such as 'A Whole New Way to Train' and 'Come to Your Senses'. There is no real entry point for the would-be swimmer who is still struggling to put their face in the water and say goodbye to the shallow end.

I think Terry is ultimately right in his philosophy. It makes perfect sense, is absolutely doable and is particularly inspiring about the potential in each and every one of us. However, I would suggest using it as an addition, rather than a starting point for the beginner. Although it would be utterly overwhelming if used alone, from scratch, none of us should miss out on his joyful recommendations on how to use the water to our advantage, to feel grace when we're in it, and to swim smart rather than simply exhaust ourselves.

Below are the basics on which both methods agree. It is essentially 'catch, pull, push' once you're moving, with three things to remember before that.

Breathing

As previously discussed, this is undoubtedly the hardest but most important part of swimming front crawl. It is not instinctive to plunge your head into water. It is not instinctive to exhale deeply when you experience a spike of anxiety. It is not instinctive to relax and become your most supple when adrenaline is coursing through your veins. But it is doable. It is well within your grasp. It is there, waiting for you to master.

There are many techniques to help you become accustomed to exhaling underwater, from simply emptying your lungs until you're sitting at the bottom of the shallow end to choosing two-syllable words to repeat underwater so that you find a rhythm. I wish I had an 'only drill you'll ever need'-type secret to pass on to you. But the truth is both more simple and more frustrating: you just have to keep at it. As with those first few childhood forays on a new bicycle, or learning to drive a car as an adult, it is only when you are good enough at each of the individual components of the stroke that the click happens and you are not thinking about what you're are doing: you're merely doing it. Decide to be relaxed, decide to practise exhaling, decide to invest a little time in working on the stroke: one day, the breathing will click.

Body position

You need to be as level as possible with the water's surface. The snag is, when you are level, you often feel as if you're swimming downhill – particularly if you are still holding air in your lungs (which can create the effect of having an inflated beach ball beneath your chest) or if you have strong, muscular legs that are more likely to naturally sink in the water.

There is one simple thing you can do to remedy this: remember to breathe out, so that your chest is not a pointless sack of air but a slick, streamlined piece of swimming majesty, letting your legs rise and your heels lightly break the surface. This will leave you more parallel to the water. The more you exhale, the more confident you will be about putting your head in the water, the better your general position will be.

But note! At all costs try not to stay in this position all the time. Good old Total Immersion Terry would have you imagine yourself as a beautiful yacht at this point, tilting from side to side at each stroke with a lovely roll. Of course, if you have one arm in the water pulling down, and one making its way up and over your head, you will slip through the water more sleekly if you're slightly on your side than if you're doggedly staying flat to the water. Terry has a point, but perhaps not one to trouble yourself with until you're a few lessons in.

Finally, don't forget your head. Yes, you will have to spend a little more time looking around if you're in open water, but for the rest of the time you need to be gazing firmly down. Your head is heavy: if you are constantly looking ahead, you will start to feel it in your neck muscles before long. (I spent a good few weeks thinking something had suddenly gone wrong with my pillows before I was told I needed to adjust my head position.) If you look down, you need only to tip your face slightly to the side when you breathe, as your head will create a beautiful bow wave ahead of you, just like that streamlined yacht Terry Laughlin likes to talk about.

Leg kick

Most people – particularly runners – will be inclined to kick from the knee as powerfully as possible once they're in the water. It gives you the sensation of keeping yourself afloat nicely, thrusting forward. Sadly, that sensation is entirely misleading. When you're swimming front crawl – particularly if you're in open, salty water, or wearing a wetsuit with plenty of added buoyancy – your legs are used as barely more than a rudder. This is almost unbearably counterintuitive for the runner-turned-swimmer, but presumably a lovely rest for a triathlete. Either way, the truth is unavoidable – kicking like a toddler having a tantrum is a tremendous waste of energy and precious oxygen for very little return. You should aim to find the most efficient way of pulling yourself along, rather than pushing your airbag lungs and big heavy head from behind.

Kick from the hip, your entire leg undulating, your ankles floppy and slightly turned in. Imagine holding a pound coin between your buttocks. You will feel your stomach and hip muscles engage as you gently tip yourself in the water, particularly if you're in a busy pool with a lot of backwash, or open water with a bit of momentum. At first, it's eerily stressful to be trying to get somewhere while using your legs as little as possible. Give yourself time – soon the floppy magic will reveal itself to you.

Catch

This refers to the angle at which your hand enters the water ahead of you, and what you do with it after that. For this part of the stroke, you want to create the biggest flat surface area, in order to have the biggest 'paddle', so that you can move as much water as possible from in front of you to behind you.

Think of your flat, downward-facing hand and the soft underside of your arm from wrist to elbow as one single paddle. A lovely long, flat paddle.

This paddle needs to enter the water fingertips first, slicing into it with your hand at about 30–45°. It then needs to keep travelling forward, underwater, reaching as far as you can. This reach, gliding forward under the surface of the water, is what will transform you from a thrashing, panicking maniac to a strong, elegant swimmer, with plenty of time to both breathe and admire the beauty of the tiny bubbles your hand makes, dancing against the light.

There are a few things to look out for with this moment of entry into the water. Do not reach too far while your hand is still above the surface. This can cause either your hand to slap down on the water, having left it too late to glide beneath it, or your elbow to flop down and hit the surface first. Imagine you were standing with both arms outstretched in front of you: ideally, the point at which your hand should enter is parallel to the area between your opposite elbow and wrist. (Unhelpfully, your other arm is not there as a guide when you're actually swimming.)

While your hand is heading for the water, you also need to be careful not to let it tip inwards, entering thumb-first. This is another of the habits I had picked up as looking very swimming-y, and spent a long time trying to shed.

Finally, you need to make sure that you keep your hands shoulder width apart. Again, when you're actually in the water, it becomes horribly easy to misjudge what your arms are doing. After all, all the action is taking place above your head. When I feel as if my arms are shoulder width apart, they are actually almost crossing each other inches in front of my head. When they really are shoulder width apart, I feel as if I'm almost spread-eagled. Countless drills with a plastic pole being held in front of me, fingers skimming first one end then the other as my arms rotated, was what trained me out of this habit, and it's still a battle to keep on top of it. It is worth the battle, though: staying nice and wide in the water is particularly useful for open-water swimming, when you'll be rolling a little too, akin to that beautiful sleek yacht, navigating the seas with grace and ease.

Once you have completed that moment of glide, and your hand has surged forward as if you were trying to ease something off a shelf just out of your reach, it is time to catch the water. If you have just completed a lovely reach, it is tempting to keep that stretched hand and to push the water down. Tempting, but wrong! Tip your wrist a little, remember that pressing the water away is what propels you forward, and make sure you move the water back behind you, not beneath you.

Pull

If you imagine the 180° semicircle that the hand and arm moves in the water from entry to exit, the catch is about the first 15° of it. The pull is the middle 90°. This is a moment where it helps to really visualise which muscles you're using: instead of just dragging your arm back from the elbow, you are using the power in your shoulder muscles to pull the water from in front of you to behind you, as you swim over it. Your hand and forearm should be working as a paddle again, your arm relatively soft at the elbow so that you clear the side of your body, taking a huge scoop of water with you.

Water is a thousand times denser than air: think how heavy a bucket of water or a large, full watering can feels in your hand. This pull through the water below you is a big, strong movement, and you want to make the most of it. Getting your hand and arm position right is key to moving efficiently, preserving precious energy and becoming a happy swimmer, but it also takes time and practice. It was only when I was videoed underwater that I realised I was moving my hand right in to below my boob before moving it back out again. It felt like a lovely big swoosh of water I was shifting; I felt like such a swimmy swimmer! But there is no point moving water in an S-curve when you could be pulling it away from you with lots of traction.

Push

The last 15° of the underwater semicircle is easy to forget. You can no longer see your hand – it's on its way towards leaving the water again – and by now your opposite hand is your focus, about to enter the water with a dynamic slice. But don't forget that hand behind you! There is still more propulsion to be had here, and simply whipping your arm out without letting it finish the stroke can leave you more tired than you need to be. Remember, it's not how many strokes you can do in a distance that counts, but the length and quality of each one. If you really use your arm, pushing the water away firmly with your hand as it draws up level to your thigh, you will eventually develop a lovely long stroke, with more time for starfish spotting and general meditative bounty.

Arm recovery

Finally, you need to lift your arm up and out of the water, ready for the next stroke. This is best done with a nice strong, engaged elbow, clearing the water around you. Some swimmers will leave their arm and hand lower, swinging it round. No one seems to have come up with any conclusive evidence that one style is better than the other, as long as the arm is engaged, not just flopping out of the water ready to slap down ahead of you. When you are tired – particularly in open water – not clearing the waves around you can cause you to judder and pause, messing with your rhythm and breathing, and only making you more tired. Training yourself to have a nice clean recovery is worth it for that moment in a swim when you start to convince yourself you're too tired to go on: this way, you'll always have a little more to give.

I can quite imagine that reading this section all in one go might send you into a spiral of anxiety and confusion. There are a lot of tiny, intricate movements here that require a level of precision combined with a degree of grit. And, of course, it all needs to be done while you're feeling delightfully relaxed. The single most important thing you need to remember is that this is within your grasp. It is not impossible, it is simply unfamiliar. Like learning a dance step, or the route for a new car journey, or simply mastering an over-elaborate TV remote, what at first seems to be an impossible amount of new information to absorb can, and will, become second nature with a little practice.

And I do appreciate that 'a little practice' is an endlessly elastic turn of phrase. To be specific: I could not swim a length, and I took a year-long course of three school terms. There were twelve lessons per term and I missed at least six of them because of illness, deadlines, and perhaps that one time I discovered that all of *30 Rock* was on Netflix. It took me about eight lessons to be able to swim. I was still not swimming terribly well, I was exhausted by the end of each lesson, and I wasn't strong, skilled or confident enough to be swimming in the sea, but I *was* swimming, with the breathing working correctly. At that point I am sure I could have joined a club and worked with a group to improve, but I was lucky enough to have a good facility at a reasonable price near my home.

Being taught as an adult can be a dizzyingly horrible prospect: it means surrendering to the fact that you can't do something, asking for help from people who don't know you, and trying something that might make you look foolish if you get it wrong. But a handful of lessons and a few hours of practice is a very small investment relative to the joy that swimming can open up to you.

A good teacher will help you with drills and demonstrations for each of the components I have described to you, building your muscle memory so that the motions start to feel seamless, as one. And once you have that muscle memory, you can pick up swimming whenever you need to, regardless of age, confidence or fitness. Yes, water is a thousand times more dense than air, but that can be a positive as well as a negative: you will avoid impact pain, feeling support from the water instead; you can learn with far lower risk of injury from falls, trips or sprains; you can exercise even when feeling weak, sad or otherwise injured.

The single best thing you can do if you want to swim well, or swim far, is to work on your stroke. I don't mean endless aggressive drills or giving yourself a hard time for being less than eel-like after a couple of months. If you focus on aerobic fitness, speed drills or muscle capacity too much or too early on, you will only build strength and fitness around bad habits and set yourself up for working hard without getting as far as you could. Sure, it can be satisfying to train hard with some cardio drills, or to do shoulder weights to build your muscle mass. But it won't hold your attention in the water over time.

Instead, you want to pursue the moment when swimming starts to feel like one continuous, flowing movement. Your arms wheeling, your heart gently pumping, your hips and shoulders rolling in synch as your core muscles stay engaged, working with the water as your mind slowly becomes soothed by the beat of your breath: that is what I mean by working on your stroke.

The purest joy that swimming offers is the delicious rhythm, the state of flow, that you can experience – particularly in open water, uninterrupted by turning. As the lovely Terry Laughlin puts it, 'Pursuit of Flow, more than the willingness to train hard, is the surest path to swimming your best. What activity could be more perfectly suited to Flow State than swimming?'

CHAPTER TWELVE

Your Body, Swimming

Our anxieties around swimming are apparently infinite. But, as Patrick told me that first day, they are not always irrational. Swimming can be dangerous, it can be terrifying, and we should exercise due caution, understanding the risks we're undertaking and working out how to overcome them. But what are myths and what are facts? And how can we most effectively help ourselves? What follows are the top ten questions that seem to come up time and time again, and the best ways to deal with them.

1. I'm worried that swimming is very dangerous – don't a lot of people drown doing it?
There are many highly valid reasons to feel anxious about swimming. People do die in the water, and often they drown. The last available annual UK statistics, from 2013, state that 381 people died in the water that year. That seems like a lot: more than one per day. After all, it only takes 2–3 pints of water to drown the lungs.

However, not all of the cases recorded were actual drownings.

Some of these people will have had existing medical conditions, or emergencies such as heart attacks that could well have taken place somewhere else; it's just that they happened to be in the water. Some will have been accidents, such as tripping and falling unconscious before reaching the water, or people jumping in when intoxicated. And then there are the risks of cold-water immersion, which I will talk about later in the chapter.

The fact remains that 381 is a scary-sounding number, and a startling one compared to many other recreational pursuits or ways of keeping fit and healthy: it is a valid reason to feel anxious about getting in the water the first few times. If you can't swim properly, don't get in unless you are in shallow water. Make sure you know how deep the pool is, or what the tides are doing. Swimming can be dangerous.

But to put it in context, 1,700 people died in car accidents that same year. That is over four times as many people, but few of us think twice about getting in a car. Everything we do is a risk to one degree or another. I believe the benefits of swimming far outweigh the risks, especially to the sober, sensible and considered swimmer.

2. Is chlorine bad for me, or will it ruin my skin, hair and nails?
There are a lot of alarming statistics available online about chlorine, but one truth is clear: chlorinated water is better for you than a pool that harbours bacteria, germs, algae and organic debris from sweat, suncream, skin and hair. Chlorine has doubtless saved lives since being used in swimming pools, and will continue to do so.

However, there is a reason why it was also used as a chemical weapon in the First World War: in high enough doses it is a vicious respiratory irritant, and in extreme cases even a few deep breaths can kill. Consequently, it can affect some people after exposure in the pool. It makes me sneeze for an hour or two after a pool swim. And it can exacerbate existing conditions such as eczema and asthma, as well as drying out skin, hair and nails. Our skin is our biggest organ, so we absorb chlorinated water all over – simply keeping our mouth, eyes and nose closed won't help.

Used properly in a pool, chlorine is not an actual danger. It's nevertheless wise to seek out a variety of swimming environments, as there are now alternative methods of keeping pool water clean and filtered. If those options are not available to you, there are ways to protect yourself. The best is to shower before getting in the pool. Covering skin and hair in fresh water makes it less absorbent to the pool water. There are also a wide variety of swimming-specific hair masks available, although I believe they tend to add to the larger problem of oil and debris in the water. Sure, your hair might become dry if you don't use the mask, but if you do use one, you're actually dunking a further dose of oil into the pool, potentially making it require further chlorine . . . and so the cycle continues. It is also wise to get fresh air as soon as possible after a pool swim, rather than staying in the closed, humid environment of the poolside.

3. Will I get injured?

Swimming deserves its reputation as an exercise that is highly unlikely to leave you injured: it is low impact, you have the support of the water, and there are no sudden jerky movements caused by other players or equipment. However, any long-term repetitive movement puts the body at risk of injury or inflammation. And for swimmers, the Achilles heel is, er, the shoulder. Specifically, it is the group of muscles and tendons that surround the shoulder joint, where the top of the arm meets the socket, known as the rotator cuff. On someone with low body fat and great muscle definition, it is quite clearly visible – the part of the shoulder that can look like wings.

Because of the angle of your arm and shoulder when you are at the most intense load-bearing part of the pull-push movement underwater, huge pressure can be put on the rotator cuff – particularly on the tendons, as they are passing through a relatively small gap. If overused, or used in the wrong position, inflammation and pain will follow. The three best things you can do for yourself to either avoid or support this type of injury are the same as for most sporting injuries: correct your technique, do some supporting exercises, and don't disrespect the concept of rest.

A slack technique – such as shoulders that stay resolutely flat against the water rather than rolling with it, or hands that enter at the wrong angle – can cause damage. It is significantly easier and cheaper to work on your stroke technique before embarking on any feats of endurance than to pay for physiotherapy to deal with the pain afterwards. Doing some dry-land exercises to build the muscles will also help. And please, remember that rest does not mean you have failed: it means you are healing, and growing.

4. Can I still swim if I've got my period?
Yes, absolutely; it's one of the main reasons why tampons were invented. And I understand that Mooncups – once you have

the hang of them – are equally good, perhaps even better, since they don't leave you with the telltale string potentially visible. I would go as far as to actively recommend swimming if you're in pain due to menstruation. Unlike running or walking, which can leave you with a thudding, heavy feeling, of gravity bearing down on you and your uterus, the weightless nature of swimming can be a blessed relief from cramps and aches. Take note, though – I have learned from bitter experience that while it is possible to walk, say, across an office or a party to the bathroom with a tampon discreetly tucked up your sleeve, this is not possible when wearing a wetsuit, herding for a pre-event Portaloo. Holding it in your hand will just have to do.

5. Isn't swimming going to hurt my ears?
Well, yes and no. Swimming can put your ears at risk of damage, but there are some simple things you can do to prevent this. There are two main problems: one helpfully known as swimmer's ear, and the other unhelpfully named surfer's ear.

Swimmer's ear (otitis externa) is an infection of the ear canal, running from the inner ear, by your eardrum, to the external part of the ear. Water can gather here, providing the perfect environment for bacteria to grow and develop. Counterintuitively, using things like cotton buds, with which you might *think* you're keeping your ears lovely and dry, can actually scrape at the skin, breaking it and providing an opportunity for more complicated infections to take root.

Conditions like this can be almost exquisitely painful. Within two months of starting my swimming course, I had a bad ear infection. The side of my face swelled up and I was convinced I had mumps. It hurt to chew food, it hurt to smile, it hurt to sleep on one side. I shudder even remembering it, but antibiotic ear drops dealt with it within a week.

What could I have done to prevent it? Well, I should have focused on drying my ears properly when I got out of the pool rather than waiting until bedtime and fiddling around with cotton buds. I would leave the water rattling around in my ears, shoving some headphones in for good measure during my journey home, and then just wait hopefully for what a friend once described to me as 'the hot trickle': the water that had been gently warming up in my ears slowly making its way out. I am retching as I type. These days I tend to put a drop of tea tree oil in my ears before swimming in a pool, and I make sure I dry them at the same time that I dry my hair – often, a quick blast with the hairdryer to double check. Also, I no longer use in-ear headphones. I have never had another ear infection.

Surfer's ear (exostosis) is an entirely different problem, and one caused exclusively by time spent in cold water. Hence the name: it is a problem that has become more prevalent since advances in wetsuits have meant surfers are able to spend much longer periods of time in the water.

Somewhat grotesquely, and for a reason no one seems to have adequately explained, cold water causes the bones that make up the ear canal to continue to grow. I know. It's like an oversight made by Dr Frankenstein. But it's true. The bone grows, the tunnel becomes narrower, and then comes the trouble hearing and the world of infections caused by the water getting stored behind the bone growth. Again, I retch.

The solution to surfer's ear is not ear drops. Far from it: it can in fact require surgery, under general anaesthesia, and the use of a small drill or chisel. I imagine that now you are armed with this information, you will develop the same sudden passion for wax earplugs that I did. Because they are the solution. Simply don't let the water in. Trust me. And don't search for this on YouTube unless you have a strong stomach.

6. Is swimming in the cold bad for me?

Regular, acclimatised swimming in cold water for reasonable periods of time is not bad for you. In fact there is an increasing amount of evidence that it can help both physical and mental health in all sorts of wonderful ways – even trivial ones such as its knack of tightening pores and flattening hair follicles for gleaming post-swim locks.

Repeated immersion in cold water is a stress-inducing non-infectious stimulus to the body: increasing metabolic rate and burning calories with the post-swim shivers; activating the immune system by increasing white blood cell count; increasing lymphatic drainage; improving the circulation and stimulating the brown fat that can lead to weight loss. Effectively, being a mild stressor keeps the whole system on its toes.

Then there are the long-term mental effects. Cold water prompts norepinephrine and endorphins – nature's painkillers, the chemicals that give us that sense of being high – to flood the body in order to help with the sting of the cold on your skin. It also stimulates the parasympathetic nervous system, decreasing the panicky fuel that is cortisol, and prompting the release of dopamine and serotonin, neurotransmitters with the effect of keeping us happy.

HOWEVER – and I would like you to picture that word in twelve-foot neon illuminated letters – the immediate effects on a body of sudden immersion in cold water are dramatic, unavoidable, and particularly powerful if you are unacclimatised. In short, it doesn't matter how fit, how strong or how young you are: for the unprepared, the effect can be catastrophically dangerous. There are, after all, only two outcomes if you are in water colder than your core body temperature: you will warm up the entire sea, river or lake to your temperature (um, unlikely); or it will cool you down to its temperature (all but guaranteed).

When you hit the water, your skin immediately cools, your outer blood vessels narrowing to conserve body heat and oxygen specifically for around the vital organs. This process, known as peripheral vasoconstriction, will cause your heart rate to rise suddenly, and your blood pressure with it. (Curiously, it can also make you feel intensely as if you need to pee.) Your breathing will become erratic within seconds, and in some cases you will over-breathe, ultimately hyperventilating as you try to get oxygen into your panicking body.

Moments later, the increased amount of carbon dioxide that you are expelling will cause painful muscle cramps, and as your blood has moved to the centre of the body, your hands, feet, arms and legs will start to become very tired, and struggle to move as well as normal. And that is just the first few minutes, in water that could be moving fast around you.

So yes, you can tell the smartarse in the pub who calls you an idiot for undertaking outdoor swimming that they are right when they say that cold water is horribly bad for you. But then you can tell them that when the body is properly acclimatised, and entry to the water is slow rather than sudden, it is also undeniably good for you.

7. I want the good effects – how do I acclimatise?

Acclimatisation is not something that can be embarked upon in a hurry. It takes, well, the whole winter, really. And you can't drift in and out of the commitment. Essentially, you have to keep entering the water as the seasons change and the water temperature drops. This way, you won't feel the drop in temperature as it happens, slowly, over many months; your body will become incrementally more tolerant of it, the water seeming almost the same temperature every day as you adapt to it. Of course, there are days when the sea is too rough, the river is too full or the lido, surrounded by sheet ice, is just unbearable, but on the whole you need to go in at least once a week to keep your body acclimatised. I swim regularly with men and women who don't even wear wetsuits, but who have developed a very keen sense of how long they can confidently swim in cold water. Some days, at the coldest time of year, it is only ten or fifteen minutes.

And don't be tricked by when the coldest water temperatures of the year actually are. The larger the body of water, the longer the lag in temperature and the more dramatic the drop. An outdoor pool or lido gets cold much faster than the ocean does, but it will also warm up much faster. The sea will retain the summer sun's heat for a good six or eight weeks, which means that swimming in October is still pleasant, even if you cracked open that first packet of opaque tights for work a fortnight ago. But the spring sunshine of late March, no matter how lovely it feels on your back in the park, takes weeks to warm the ocean.

Consequently, March is generally the coldest month for outdoor swimming, but it is eminently doable if you keep your tolerance up. I managed about twenty minutes most days, wearing a half-wetsuit (arms in, legs out) and no gloves or neoprene hat. Sometimes it was forty minutes if the sun was on my side, and those in my group who wear full wetsuit, socks, gloves and hat were happily swimming for up to forty-five minutes, several times a week, at about 6°.

It is important to note that we are all healthy swimmers who had taken a specific sea swimming course and who committed ourselves to swimming regularly and never unaccompanied. We also retained fitness by doing other sport on the days that we could not swim in the sea, whether it was pool swimming, running or even gardening. If you have existing cardiovascular or circulation problems, you should not attempt cold-water swimming unless you have had the most serious of discussions with your doctor. And you can't make it a New Year's resolution and hurl yourself off a boat on 1 January. It is simply not possible to will the basics of thermodynamics away in a moment of high spirits.

8. Okay, I'm up for it – but how do I warm up again afterwards?
You would not be unreasonable to assume that it's as simple as 'have a hot shower and pop on a bobble hat', but it isn't: the moment you leave the water, the peripheral vasoconstriction ends. Cold blood from your extremities is pumped around the body, mixing with the warm blood that was around your core. As the switch happens, regardless of your outdoor environment and even though your overall body temperature is increasing, your core body temperature drops. It takes about 10–15 minutes for this switch in temperature to occur, at which point you feel a deep cold within, and the shivers kick in. This sensation of delayed inner chill is call 'the after-drop', and is both unnerving and invigorating.

The most important thing to know about getting warm is that you should do it from the inside out. Don't get into a steaming hot shower or bath ten minutes after leaving the sea, but do have a hot drink or some warm food. External heat will speed up the movement of the cooled blood, making the after-drop more severe, and possibly causing you to faint. Warm food or drink won't.

Make the most of the minutes between exiting the water and the after-drop kicking in. Sure, your hands might be a bit stiff from the cold, but bung on as many clothes as you can before the shivers start – they make it near impossible to deal with buttons, zips and laces. Since warm food or drink will help both your hands and your heart, make sure you're prepared with either a flask or a café nearby.

And don't be impatient – trying to drive or cycle as your core body temperature drops and the shakes kick in is optimistic at best, damn foolish at worst. Keep an eye on the others you swam with, enjoy the snacks and let nature take its course. In ten minutes you'll feel a furnace burning within you for the rest of the day.

9. Is swimming going to help me lose weight, because it always leaves me so hungry?
Currently there is no absolute consensus on what it is about swimming that makes us so hungry, but most scientists agree that it is connected to two things: the change in body temperature created even by pool swimming, and the deceptive nature of being surrounded by water that makes us forget we're sweating, thirsty and therefore getting dehydrated.

Even standard indoor swimming pools are a lower temperature than our body core, so any swimming will make our internal organs work a little harder at temperature regulation, alongside all of the other cardiovascular and muscular activity going on. Some scientists believe that the temperature change while in the water dulls hunger, making it return with a vengeance once we're out, while others claim it triggers a hunger response that our body doesn't realise is temporary. Still others believe that it is simply the extra energy it takes to handle even mild peripheral vasoconstriction that makes us hungrier than running or other sports would.

Either way, combined with the dehydration we so often fall for, our post-swim hunger is often far greater than our actual post-swim need for food. Infuriating! This is then added to the fact that the more streamlined and efficient your stroke is, the less energy you will actually need to expend to move through the water, and so the fewer calories you will burn on a regular swim. This is great if you want to get from A to B, or to win a race, but less good if you're trying to actively shed weight.

The combination of these factors perhaps explains why swimming sometimes has a bad reputation for making us put on weight. The reputation is wildly undeserved, if understandable. I would also like to suggest that it doesn't matter. Sure, we should all try to stay within the healthy weight range for our age and height, but it is far from necessary to conform to the media, advertising industry and social media's idea of what a 'swimmer' looks like.

10. What about the terror? You know, the terror of bumping into a fish, a seal, a jellyfish or an as-yet-unspecified terrifying sea monster lurking in the dark?
I know the terror. The mind can be cruel. As I discussed in Chapter 4, what is going on inside your head can have an

immediate and enormous effect on what goes on in your body. So the terror – whether of learning to swim for the very first time, or of setting off in an open-water event in an unfamiliar watery environment – is real, and can be dangerous. The slow, creeping thoughts about what might be nearby, the endless darkness below you and the distance between you and the shoreline or riverbank can leave you panting, panicking and petrified if you don't master a few simple steps to take control of the situation.

- Make sure that your wetsuit, if you're wearing one, fits well and has been put on properly. Twisted neck and shoulder lines can mean that your emotional sense of claustrophobia is increased by an actual sense of being restricted. Get used to wearing your wetsuit for short swims where you feel entirely comfortable or are supported by official lifeguards before you take on anything bigger.

- Enter the water slowly and calmly. Whether it's a pool or open water, hurling yourself in when you're prone to being nervous will only sharpen your breath. And cold water will do this to a far greater degree. Wade into open water slowly, forcing yourself to exhale as you do. Tip your face into the water while you can still touch the bottom; only once your breath has regulated should you set off swimming.

- Don't start too fast. Even if you're in an event and aiming for a good time, don't be conned into thinking that the buoyancy of the wetsuit means you won't need to warm up your heart and lungs once you start moving. Being a little short of breath for the first five or ten minutes is entirely normal as your heart rate quickens and your lungs get to work, but darting off at top speed will not give you a chance to steady your breathing and could lead to even bigger panic.

- Rest if you need to. If you're in the pool, there is no shame in taking a breather in the shallow end to calm your mind. And in open water, you always have the option to take good old Everard Digby's advice and flip yourself onto your back for a moment. If you're in a wetsuit, you will float with little or no effort, so you can gather your thoughts. Switching to breaststroke or simply slowing down a little may also work for you.

- Get to know your neighbours. You are more likely to feel relaxed about what is lurking in the water if you actually find out what *is* lurking in the water. You will never be able to know for sure, but a little research into what is around you will at least provide distraction from the worst your imagination can come up with, and ought to give you a little reassurance at least.

CHAPTER THIRTEEN
Swimsuits and Beyond

From wetsuits to nose plugs and everything in between, there is almost no limit on the amount of gear you can buy for swimming, particularly if you're going to commit to swimming in open water and equipping yourself for year-round adventures. But it is worth doing your research before buying everything presented to you as a potential lifesaver. After all, swimming is one of the most democratic forms of exercise available to us: you don't even need a swimming costume to plunge into a local lake, sea or river.

Swimming costumes

A note on swimming costumes: one of the main reasons people give me for not wanting to swim is, frankly, not wanting to be in a swimming costume. Research done by Sport England backs up the fact that it is one of the primary factors stopping people, specifically women, getting into the water. I know those fears, I know those dark days, I know the overwhelming sensation that you're not the right shape for Lycra, that you aren't like the models on the swimwear website or in the shop, that people will look disparagingly at you in your costume. And I've only found one way to get over it: to put on a swimming costume, again and again and again, until it stops feeling like exposure and starts feeling like freedom. I stare at myself in the mirror and tell myself that in five years' time I will kill to look like this. When I was fifteen, I thought I was chubby, but when I was twenty, I looked back and saw that I'd been lovely . . . and so it has continued for nearly twenty years.

It is not your responsibility to feel more confident or to be more fabulous. It is everyone else's responsibility to respect the shape and size that you choose to be, and for us all to extend that courtesy to each other. The variety of shapes, sizes and weights is both enormous and magnificent, and hanging out in swimwear will make that more obvious. Whether you wish there were less of your hips, more of your boobs or fewer of your wrinkles, no one else in the world is seeing what you see, because they can't access your inner monologue, your hang-ups and your worries. They're too busy thinking about their own. Unless they're a long-term swimmer. Because there's a secret that long-term swimmers often keep to themselves, hugging it close to their hearts as they huddle and shiver around that cup of tea: the more time you spend in swimwear, the less you actually care what you look like in it.

Well, I'm happy to share. It's what we see and what we do in swimwear that matters to swimmers. If you're in a bikini three times a week, feeling the water around you, acknowledging the fish below you and watching the birds dancing above you, you have redefined what a bikini body is: it's your body, in a bikini. You feel weightless in the water, and as time passes it is that inner sense of how much you feel you weigh rather than any external perceptions about your size or shape that starts to matter more. And then you are free, floating like the swimmer who has just kicked off from the shore, feeling dry land and its tedious judgements pulling away behind them. Anything is possible.

Let's get shopping.

Advising people on what swimming costume to buy is a little bit like advising potential runners on running shoes: ultimately, the most important thing is going to be that you feel positive enough about yourself in it that you will want to wear it and get swimming. The variety of colours, shapes and styles out there is magnificent and apparently infinite, and truly there is something for everyone. I won't try to guide you on what you need or what you should look like, as frankly I think swimsuits are only needed for decency's sake anyway. They provide little practical benefit beyond not getting you arrested, and even then some swimmers will take that risk in order to feel the water truly surround their body!

The only practical considerations you need to bear in mind are that suits with a 'sporty' or 'racer' cross-back style are terrifying to get into if you have a bottom wider than your shoulders, but are incredibly comfortable for front crawl once you're in them; and that what feels uncomfortable as you walk to the pool – gravity working against you – might feel delicious once you are horizontal, moving in the water with gravity on your side. I have two swimming costumes that are unbearable out of the water, constantly riding up if I wear them for more than about eight minutes, but a perfect fit once I'm in and moving. It took time to work this out, and now I simply don't wear them to the pool or on the beach: they're business only.

Given these rather lax boundaries, I am confident that there is a swimming costume for everyone out there. There are modest suits, similar to the Edwardian bathing style, that cover hips and bums. There are extra-long suits for the lengthy of torso. There are post-surgery suits for those fresh from either a mastectomy or prior gender transition surgery. There are suits with tummy-tightening fabric to help you to feel supported after having a baby. There are suits with bra inserts, suits with temporary padded inserts to combat over-assertive nipples, and tankinis for those who don't want to be held back by a one-piece. The best, most affordable of many of these things are available globally at M&S.

There are burqinis for those who choose to wear them for religious reasons (also M&S), suits that cover your entire body if you want to avoid the sun (from labels such as Coverswim), high-end brands that make sturdy, sporty styles in fabulous neons, and technical suits that promise to shave seconds off your time. Truly, whatever you are looking for, it is out there. Just remember this: the sizing for each and every one of these items will be erratic.

I am pretty much a standard size 12. I have some clothes that are larger, the consequence of a year of IVF treatment. And I have some clothes that are smaller. But I know that I am not an XXL. Nevertheless, Sweaty Betty sizing tells me that I am: I have a couple of beautiful swimming costumes by them that I have had to buy in XXL in order to fit over my body. On the one hand: fine, I don't care what size they say I am! On the other: having vowed to begin exercising, I spent years never getting further than the changing room, as it just left me so sad to be told I was too big for the nice stuff. I've spent enough time observing this industry to know that I don't care any more if I'm the biggest at a sportswear event. But I wonder if some of those brands know how many people are put off exercise by that kind of sizing, or whether they're simply not bothered. How many other women never reach the water because their experience in the changing room was too depressing?

Please don't be one of them!

Either buy online or go armed for swimwear shopping: take a bottle of water, take extra underwear, and take your time. Try on four times more costumes than you feel like, because then you'll never have to come back. Try not to think about whether you look acceptable, slim-sexy, or swimmer-y enough. Imagine yourself gliding through the water, weightless and supported, floating on your back looking down over yourself and enjoying the sight.

Wetsuits

Wetsuits have two main purposes: to keep you warm, and to keep you buoyant. They work wonderfully at both, but do require the potential lonely agony of finding one that fits. And a wetsuit that doesn't fit is worth nothing at all, so it is worth investing a bit of time and energy in getting it right. Helpfully, you don't have to buy a wetsuit immediately. There are many places that make them available for hire – either for a specific event or to let you try one out for fit and comfort. Often companies let you hire a wetsuit first with a view to keeping it and buying it. Good places to look into wetsuit hire in the UK are www.mywetsuithire.co.uk, www.greatswim.thetristore. com and www.triuk.com.

Wetsuit types

Wetsuits for swimmers and surfers are slightly different. Surfers do not need as much upper-body flexibility, and are less constantly aerobic in the water (a lot of lying around on boards, looking dashing), so their suits are generally thicker. Surfing wetsuits are about 5mm+ in thickness, and can be quite cumbersome to try and do consistent swimming in.

Swimming wetsuits, often sold as triathlon suits, are generally thinner, or a mix of thicknesses. Some are as little as 2mm in areas such as around the shoulders, but thicker around the vital organs. And unlike surfers' wetsuits, they are designed not to make your legs so buoyant that they pop up above the surface of the water, leaving you kicking the air or unable to do breaststroke. Swimmers' wetsuits are also coated with a slick external layer that reduces the drag in the water (and makes you feel like an otter).

I love my full wetsuit, and have always felt very comfortable in it. But I have only worn it a handful of times, for events. I was still in just my swimming costume well into October, and for the coldest months of winter I have worn a half-wetsuit, which is designed for surfers. It has none of the coating or slick design of a swimmer's wetsuit, and is simply a swimming costume made of neoprene, but with long sleeves. It is from a brand called Neon, and I bought it in a surfwear shop in Covent Garden when I spotted it in a sale. It isn't slick, and the surf fabric gives a little too much drag to wear it in an unheated pool, but I adore it. I love having my legs out in the water, and I am definitely planning to invest in a second suit, this time with no arms. I confess that I don't know anyone else who does this, though. Everyone else I swim with is in proper wetsuits or swimming costumes!

Brands

There are all sorts of swimming wetsuit brands, such as Blue Seventy, Orca, Speedo, Snugg, Zone 3 and 2XU. I have no particular preference, and I have never managed to establish among the swimmers I know whether there is any particularly excellent brand or one to avoid. This is because the most important thing is not the pink and purple squiggles up the outer thighs, or the seconds that it can shave off your race time, but whether it fits you and fits you properly.

Online, wiggle.co.uk is a good place to get an overview of what is available, and *H2Open* magazine (which is also available online) has a good selection of reviews and advertisements.

Fit

When you've never tried a wetsuit on before, it is completely impossible to tell whether or not the thing fits as it is supposed to. They are by nature quite uncomfortable when you're out of the water, but with good reason: the way they work is by trapping water between you and the neoprene of which they are made. A thin trickle of water creeps in at the neck, wrists and ankles as you first enter the sea, lake or river, and is then supposed to stay there, warmed by your blood temperature, protecting you from the colder water on the outer side of the suit. Consequently, a wetsuit that is too big (i.e. one that feels lovely and comfortable when you're standing around in a shop chatting) is going to let in a constant icy stream of water as you're trying to swim. Grim, exhausting, and why you should always go for a wetsuit that feels somewhat claustrophobic when you initially try it on.

But be warned! Don't go for one that is too small either – the fabric should be flush to your curves, dipping in the small of your back (if it is stretched across it, it will create a pocket for cold water). It shouldn't be too tight around the neck, either. A wetsuit that fits perfectly everywhere else but chafes every time you need to breathe will prove a waste of money, since swimming in it will be miserable and you will either end up not swimming or replacing the wetsuit.

Shops, either on- or offline, should have a chart that will show your height, weight and measurements and how they correspond to sizes. If you are extreme in any direction, there are places that make bespoke wetsuits, but they do cost approximately twice as much as off-the-peg ones.

How to get it on

The aforementioned tightness required of wetsuits makes them the most traumatic of all equipment to put on. At best, they're a time-consuming faff. At worst, they can trap you in what feels like a prison of your own flesh, and leave you sweating and exhausted before you so much as dip a toe in the water.

The main thing to remember is that you cannot rush the

process of putting a wetsuit on: you have to start at the bottom and go up inch by inch. Trying to bend forward and hook your shoulders in as you would a hairdresser's gown will leave the entire middle area bunched and inflexible, and since the coating on swimming wetsuits is delicate, you'll be at risk of ripping that as well.

First of all, put on your swimming costume. This is another layer of warmth, and it means that if you're taking the wetsuit off in public, you will have something underneath it to protect your modesty. Next, take a deep breath and pick up the wetsuit. It sounds daft, but it's a great idea to pop a couple of plastic bags on your feet before putting the wetsuit on. This will ensure that your feet and lower legs slide right down without catching on any of the fuzzy inner fabric, meaning you've already done a few inches. To get the rest of the leg on, pinch the fabric between the side of your thumb and the middle of your forefinger and inch it up until you've got it over your hip and bottom. Do not, no matter how tempting it is, grab your upper thighs with your fingers splayed like a bear claw and drag: you will be left with four half-moon nail marks in the wetsuit, which will itself have remained stationary.

Make sure that you are fully wearing the bottom half of the wetsuit, like a pair of trousers with a strange elaborate belt, before you even think about putting your arms in. Once you do, again make sure that you yank with thumb and forefinger rather than grabbing wildly at the shoulders. Eventually, make sure that you pull up the fabric at the top of your shoulders (where you'd pat yourself on the back, if you were so inclined). Finally, once everything is in place, try and zip it up. Wetsuit zips have a long enough cord attached that you can usually pull it from quite high above your head, in a much more comfortable position than if you were trying on a dress with a discreet zip. Once it's up, don't forget to tap the hitherto mysterious square of Velcro at the end of the cord onto the small dot somewhere at the bottom of the zip, around the small of your back: this will keep the cord from floating around and brushing against you, convincing you that you've swum into a swarm of jellyfish. You're in!

When to wear

Wear your wetsuit when you want to. Some people feel comforted by the buoyancy and wear them year round if they're in unheated water; others despise them and will only wear them if taking part in an organised event that stipulates that they are compulsory. Then there are many who decide what to wear depending on how long they want to swim: whether they want a quick blast of the cold or a decent forty-five minutes' exercise.

Budget

It is possible to get a decent wetsuit for around £100 and for it to last several years. There are technical advantages to more expensive ones, but prices can ascend pretty steeply. It is always worth checking on eBay or in Facebook groups for swimmers and triathletes, as there is a healthy market in wetsuits bought either as optimistic Christmas presents for loved ones who never use them, or by people who can afford to wear one a handful of times before trading up to this season's style. It is much more hygienic than buying second-hand trainers, and can be a nifty alternative to hiring, especially if you then sell on.

Care

Make sure that you rinse your wetsuit out after every single swim. Chlorine and salt water will corrode the fabric, leaving it either stiff and unusable or coming apart at the seams. I usually turn mine inside out as I take it off, then wash it in the shower with me. Be careful only to use water-based lubricants around the neck and shoulders, and to wash off any suncream or hair products that may have got onto it, as they'll rot the neoprene. Once clean, coated swimming wetsuits dry faster inside out, as this exposes the more porous fabric. Be careful not to dry them near direct heat or leave them in very hot sunlight for too long. And beware long nails and intricate jewellery near that fabric! (See below for what to do if you do create a snag.) If you're travelling with your wetsuit, try to roll it up to avoid creases in the coating.

Swimming caps

I didn't own a swimming cap until I started doing front crawl, as my delicate breaststroke days were largely motivated by keeping my head out of the water, which meant I never needed one. But if you're swimming any other stroke, they are essential – largely because you'll want to be able to both breathe and see without a veil of hair across your face. Added bonuses are warmth in cold water, protection from the effects of chlorine and salt water on your hair.

There are four basic fabrics for swimming caps, and each has its merits. I have a beloved favourite – silicone – but that is as much because of my hair length as anything else. Hair type and personal preference are the biggest factors here. Those with very long or very curly hair will need to buy caps specifically for that type of hair, and those with very short hair may find themselves wanting extra warmth while swimming outdoors.

There is also a healthy market still out there for fabulous retro swimming caps – soft rubber bubble fabric in candy colours, basic caps covered in a veritable meadow of nylon flowers, and ruched and ruffled creations are all two or three clicks away online. None are ideal for swimming front crawl, so I have stuck to the more practical here.

Rubber latex

These are generally the cheapest caps, and the most widely available in public swimming pools and online. I am not a fan, though. The latex, while being excellent at staying put once on, can be pretty uncomfortable if it slips or slides, and is almost always painful to take off. The material clings to your hair in a quite alarming way – great for stability, less great if you don't like the feeling of your hair being ripped out from the root. They can also tear very easily, which is a pain if you only carry one cap at a time and you're the sort of person who shoves such things in your handbag with keys and pens, or indeed if you have a fingernail that is anything less than perfectly filed. Oh, and don't dry a cap of this sort in the sun, because it will either melt or, as has happened to me, leave its logo on your coffee table/laptop case/kitchen counter.

If asked to wear one for an organised event or course (which you often are, so that stewards or timekeepers can tell what speed or distance group you're in), I now put the latex cap on top of my own silicone one, a system that has yet to fail me.

Silicone

Silicone is a price step up from basic latex, but is easily my preferred material. It's stretchier, more durable and incomparably easier on the hair and hairline. I find silicone caps genuinely comfortable – and they have the added advantage of being easily available online in larger 'long hair' sizes if that's what you need. But be warned! They can slip off hair that has conditioning oil or treatment on it, so make sure you pull the cap right down on to your face. They can also slip off bald heads, as I found out when swimming behind a group of men in the River Arun event. Anxious to protect the river wildlife, I shoved the ones I found up the legs of my wetsuit. All very worthy, but in the finish-line photographs I look as if I have catastrophic varicose veins.

The other advantage silicone gives me is warmth. I wore two caps together during winter's coldest months and felt no need for anything else. They are also available in a bobble design, which retains more heat. They shouldn't cost you more than about £7 at most, which still works out cheaper than a neoprene cap. A favourite brand for me is the tiny independent Under Aqua, which has lovely designs and is working on a range for longer hair, as well as other accessories.

Neoprene

Neoprene caps are for long-distance cold-water outdoor swimming. Neoprene, the fabric that wetsuits are made of, is thicker and a far better insulator than either rubber or latex, and these caps usually come with a thin chin strap to keep them on. I have never felt the need for one, as I have pretty thick hair, but several of my local swimming friends wouldn't be without theirs, particularly the ones who swim for up to forty-five minutes at a time even in the coldest weather. I suggest you only invest in one of these if that's the standard you're aiming for, as they are significantly more expensive than other caps on the market. They do create a charming 1930s Riviera chic, though. Very Grace Kelly in *High Society*.

Nylon

Nylon caps are often worn under others, as they're the softest of all on the hair. They don't have great grip, though, so if you're going any great distance, or swimming in choppy water, they may not be ideal. The seams and the cloth-like fabric can make you look a tiny bit like a bank robber who's put a pair of tights on his head only to lose the legs part. It is worth noting that they are the most environmentally friendly option, given that they use so much less plastic.

Socks and gloves

My neoprene socks absolutely changed my swimming life, and I can honestly say that I don't think I would even have made it to the water's edge if I hadn't had a pair for my first winter outdoors. And they are the cheapest item of swimming kit I own! Mine are 3mm neoprene ankle socks with no other bells or whistles, but – and it's an important but! – I was advised to buy a size smaller than I would for normal socks, and that is advice I pass on to you. Nothing will slow and frustrate you more, especially if you're cold and want to keep moving, than a pair of socks that balloon with water and make kicking and manoeuvring yourself feel harder than it needs to be. What is really important is the seam around your ankle – as with wetsuits, if the socks are hard to get on and off, you've bought the right size. When it comes to entering and exiting the water, I would never have had the nerve to tread over the sharp rocky edges of a tarn without mine, nor the stomach to squelch through the mud and roots on the side of a lake. But with my seven-quid socks on, I feel invincible.

The situation is pretty much the same for gloves – you want neoprene, and you want a good fit. Be careful buying online, though, as you don't want to take a wrong turn and end up with either webbed training gloves (more of which later) or very thick gloves designed for fishermen or windsurfers, who don't have their hands ploughing through the water constantly.

Gloves can also come with wrist straps, and it can take a few goes before you get the perfect alignment of wetsuit/glove/strap/tracking device, so don't blow the budget on a dream pair the week before a big swim; give yourself the chance to try it all on together before you need to get in the water.

There are more advanced versions of both socks and gloves – some hardier swimmers who are regularly treading more rugged terrain choose to wear small neoprene shoes that look like slippers, with rubberised bottoms and a pull cord to keep them tight. They're great if your journey to the water is adventurous, or you want something you can wear for water sports too, but they're not the most comfortable for a long swim. Similarly, getting a pair of touch-sensitive gloves so that you can answer your phone at a moment's notice is probably not worth the extra cash unless you're a doctor on call.

Goggles

If I were forced to forgo all items of kit except one, I would choose to save my goggles every time. As with all exercise, it's not what you look like to others that is important, but what you see when you're out there moving – and it's your goggles that let you see. By protecting your eyes from salt water, chlorine and bright sunlight, they enable visibility whatever the conditions. Whether it's the clock at the end of the pool, the jetty at the edge of the lake, or the fish at the bottom of the ocean, it's always worth being able to see what is important or inspiring to you, so it's crucial to get your goggles right.

The most important thing to remember about goggles is that they do not need to feel tight in order to be working effectively. The nature of the rubbery suction surround is that it's working best when simply resting on your face. In fact, when you're trying them on, out of the water, you should be able to simply rest the goggles on your face for a good 10-20 seconds with the seal intact. Indeed, it's best to try them on without relying on the straps for guidance. If you press, pull and tighten the lenses and straps, you're simply creating tension that is more likely to break the seal if the position of your face changes. I did not understand this. For a long time. Long enough to associate goggles with pain and inconvenience for the best part of a year. Don't do what I did: instead, invest a little time and perhaps some trial and error in getting a pair that will sit happily on your face for a good uninterrupted hour or two in the water. Don't suffer like I did: to want well-fitting eyewear is not an overambitious goal – the dream pair is out there!

What you want are goggles that fit your face shape and the size of your eye socket. Some seals sit right on the curve of your skeletal structure, and that is never going to work. Some swimmers prefer to feel the seal right in the eye socket; others like them up as far as their eyebrows and down as far as their cheeks. Back when I was eternally fiddling with straps, in a state of ever-tightening panic, I loved the large Aquasphere Vista style because they didn't leave my eye sockets red raw. I now swear by the Zoggs Predator Flex, as do most swimmers I know. They are particularly good at bending, from the nose, to sit well on the sides of the face – perfect for those who don't have a wide, flat face.

The goggles I wish I was cool enough to wear are the small, mirrored Swedish style that require individual assembly. They have no seal at all, only plastic lenses that come all the way around the side of the eye, and are held together by a latex nose and head strap. They allow for better peripheral vision, they come in cool colours, and they make you look like a steampunk superhero, but they are also prone to much more leakage in the water.

Second only to leakage is the annoyance of goggles fogging up. This condensation is caused by the difference in temperature between goggles, water and face. There are various techniques people use to prevent this – some hold their goggles in the water for ten or twenty seconds to bring the temperature of the two together. This is particularly recommended if your goggles are especially cold from the journey to the water, though it's also worth making sure that your face is not too hot as well. There are plenty of anti-fog sprays on the market, but most people who use anything on the lenses swear by a tiny, tiny dab of baby shampoo. This creates a very thin film across the lens that prevents the condensation from settling. My chosen technique has proven both cheap and infallible: spit. Some people actually spit into the lens, but I prefer simply to lick around it.

Vaseline/wetsuit lubricant

Salt water stings. Salt water rubbing against a seam over time takes stinging and ratchets it up to a previously unimagined level of pain. Vaseline will always be your friend if you're in a swimsuit. Suncream provides its own barrier between skin and salt water, but over time, and under intense sun, it simply isn't enough. If you're going on a swimming trip, take a tub of Vaseline, as well as a separate pair of rubber or latex gloves for applying it with. The last thing you want is to protect yourself from the abrasions of salt water only to smear grease across your goggles a moment later. Very long-distance swimmers also use lanolin or Aquaphor.

Wetsuit lubricant is easier to apply, generally coming in a sort of stick or tube akin to roll-on deodorant. It is used on the seams, particularly around the neck and underarm area, where there is most movement when you are in the water. Vaseline is not ideal for use on rubber as it can cause perishing, but using some sort of lubricant is worth it as the repeated turning of your head, for example, will cause chafe marks at your hairline over a period of time.

Liquid rubber

It sounds disgusting and it smells even worse, but this is a product that can significantly lengthen the life of your wetsuit. The biggest brand is Black Witch, and it comes in cute cartoony packaging with what looks disconcertingly like Meg of *Meg and Mog* fame on the tube. It is as magic as anything Meg ever did, as it can repair snags and scratches on coated wetsuits. If, like me, you find that getting a wetsuit on requires significant thigh-level yanking, there is a very real chance that one day you will put your fingernail through the neoprene coating. This is extremely annoying – not merely aesthetically, but because once the rubber is compromised, the chance of cold water getting into the suit is hugely increased. Usually what happens is that a small slice of coating peels back from the wetsuit, and remains there, flapping about.

Liquid rubber can mend this – you simply need to take a matchstick, cotton bud or similarly sized tool, and dip it into the tube. You don't need a lot; a blob the size of a match head is plenty. You spread the liquid into the underside of your gouge and wait for it to turn opaque – slightly white, like false eyelash glue. This is your cue to smooth the coating down, fitting it back into the slot from which it was originally ruptured and using any oozing leftovers as an extra seal. Ta-da! Your wetsuit lives to see another day. It is worth noting that an adaptation of this technique can be used to mend seams that have come unstitched. It is messier, and you need to create a lovely smooth edge to avoid chafing, but it certainly keeps the wetsuit together.

Tow floats

These look like bright neon flotation devices but should not be mistaken as such; they are – and have been tested as – bags and bags alone. Waterproof and inflatable, with a large sealed pocket for a swimmer's possessions, they vary in size. The smallest can just about squeeze in a phone, a key and tenner; while the largest are roomy enough for an entire outfit. You fill and seal the sack, then inflate the front and back pouches around it and attach it via a cord around the waist. And *voilà*, it is ready to be pulled effortlessly along behind you in the water. Mine sits somewhere around my feet once I'm swimming, and I'm only aware of it when I occasionally touch the cord with a toe. There is no sense of drag. I love my tow float, but I have found that swimmers are divided on their merits.

One of the arguments against tow floats is that they create a false sense of security in the water – you can assume you're visible to passing boats, water-skiers and fishermen, as well as to lifeguards. You also have the sensation that there is a buoyancy aid in the water with you, in case of incident or danger. Also, their bright colour can upset some of the very hardiest of outdoor swimmers, who find them a harsh interruption to the natural landscape.

Provided you accept the limitations of the tow float as a safety aid, and are well aware that that is not its designed purpose, they make fantastically useful bags – with the added bonus of some increased visibility. Sure, the organic nature of outdoor swimming is compromised if we're dragging mobile phones, route trackers and a full change of clothes with us every time. Part of swimming's attraction is the sense of weightless freedom in the water. But – and it's a big but – a lot of us don't like swimming back and forth over a long distance. Whether it's upstream, against the tide or simply the psychological sense of turning back into your own wake, heading home the way you came can sometimes take a little joy from an outdoors swim. With a tow float, you can take a pair of flip-flops, some light clothing, some change and a key with you, and return home on dry land.

Event jackets

Designed for swimmers, surfers and all cold-water enthusiasts, these items tread a fine line between being wonderfully useful and a waste of money. They range from towelling robes – adult versions of the sort of poncho children wear on the beach when they're fresh out of the water – to more durable waterproofed versions. Their websites and marketing material will try to convince you of their advanced windproof technology or powerful drying capabilities, but the main advantage of all of them is the same: they afford you a level of dignity and protection from the elements when you're getting changed out of swimwear on the beach, round the side of a harbour or behind your car in a Lake District car park.

A towelling robe is great for summer – you can pop it on over your head and rub yourself dry without looking like a niche burlesque act, sliding your swimwear down and pulling your warm clothes on with relative decorum. The waterproof versions are made of much sturdier stuff, and have an appropriately sturdy price tag. These usually zip up the front, so you can also wear them waterside before or between swims. They are much more specific to cold-water swimmers, as the thick waterproof coating (over a sort of fleecy inner layer that sits against the skin) does a great job of protecting you from wind, rain and spray from waves breaking close to the shore.

While the towelling robes, of which the brand leader is Robie Robes, create a playful, childlike look and feel, the waterproof ones – allowing for the double layer and space to change beneath them – are enormous. The brand leader here is Dryrobe, although cheaper alternatives are available online. Unzipped, they can make the wearer look regal, intimidating and a bit daft: a sort of grey, watery hip-hop superstar draped in furs. That you can get branded versions makes it worse – or better, depending on your perspective.

Once, at a supposedly fun community cold-water swimming event, I saw a gang of middle-aged white men wearing event jackets in their team colours and aggressively discussing tactics. I find these 'must get all the kit' believers a bit ridiculous; personally, I am often happier in a bin liner and a moth-eaten jumper, since I don't mind it getting filthy should I drop it on the pebbles. At that particular event, these competitive chaps were all put in the shade by a lady who had simply sewn two large swimming towels together and stitched a hem around a piece of elastic at one end. The towels appeared to date from about 1987, and even then the mauve and avocado tones suggested they were bin-ends at the House of Fraser sale. She was wearing her creation over one shoulder, looking like Michelle Pfeiffer in *Scarface*, and looked blissfully happy. Once the event started, she casually beat several of those owners of bespoke robes. Expensive post-swim kit might be deliciously comfortable, but it doesn't guarantee an unbeatable swimming style.

Floats

Back when I believed my legs were the key to successful swimming, I spent hours going up and down pools, kicking hard. Since I became enlightened, discovering that the leg kick is more of a rudder and a spare engine than the main machine, I don't feel any need for a float. Most pools have them, should you fancy a bit of leg work and are not appalled by the bite marks of small children who have used them before you.

Pull buoys

I spent years calling these 'pool boys', enchanted by their cheeky name but clueless as to what they were for. Once informed, I found them one of the most useful training tools of the lot. They are essentially floats for your legs, to help you train your arms. But where standard rectangular floats let your legs fall into the water, these wedge between them, helping to keep them high and in the position you should always be swimming in. This in turn helps you to focus on your arm stroke without struggling to keep parallel to the water. They also slow you down slightly, allowing you to work out the intricacies of what to do with your arms while stopping you from getting too breathless. If you swim in a pool that doesn't have them, I'd recommend buying one for training. And if you swim in a pool that does have them ... now you know what they do.

Fins

Shorter than the flippers you would use for swimming in the sea, swim fins are another fantastic tool for the learner swimmer. They are usually used for training drills when you're learning one specific part of the stroke, such as how you lift your arm from the water or where you position your hand as it enters the water. The fins allow you to keep moving while doing what is effectively only half a stroke, when without them you would probably start sinking. But beware: after half a lesson spent bombing up and down the pool convinced that you've nailed it, the let-down when you take them off for some 'real' swimming can be harsh.

Hand paddles and webbed gloves are also available, although they are more of a training than a learning aid, as they don't really help with buoyancy or forward movement in the same way that a pair of fins can. Instead, they are designed for creating more resistance in the water, in order to strengthen arm and shoulder muscles.

Ear drops and ear plugs

Ear drops can be useful for swimming, in either the pool or outdoors, but if you are going to swim in cold water, ear plugs are absolutely essential. Prolonged, regular exposure to cold water can cause real damage to the ear (see chapter 12).

Swimming ear drops are designed to create a thin lubricant barrier along the ear canal to prevent bacteria in the water from taking root, and some claim to clear up the water after swims, too. There are several brands, from Swim Seal and Swim-eze to Earol, which smells very strongly of tea tree oil. The main ingredients in almost all of these are olive oil (for the barrier) and alcohol (for drying). While it's nice to get a product that you can squirt satisfyingly into your ear before or after a swim, many swimmers simply dab in rum, or vodka, and olive oil. Don't tell anyone I told you that, though.

I find ear plugs for swimming largely terrifying, as so many of them seem to have a great long root that looks as if it could easily burrow into my brain. I wince at the thought of using them. The ones I prefer are silicone blobs that can be moulded to the individual ear shape. In the packet they look disconcertingly like a tray of spat-out chewing gum, but they are my recommendation to you.

Flip-flops and verruca socks

The better use you make of the former, the less you will find yourself having to use the latter. When I am pool swimming, my flip-flops do not leave my feet until I'm getting into the water, and they go straight back on upon exit. They're pretty useless on pebbly beaches, slippery river beds and rocky tarns, but invaluable if you want to avoid catching a verruca indoors.

Please, if you use a public pool, wear flip-flops as much as possible. The glory days of the 1980s, when children weren't allowed to enter a public pool unless they had first walked through a tiny trough of TCP, may be over, but the memory lingers on. Verrucas are still out there, and they still hurt – especially if you end up with one on a spot where either your running shoes or your favourite heels rub. So do your best to keep yourself and others away from them!

Water bottle

If you don't have one, you'll forget that you need to drink. Being surrounded by water makes us overlook the fact that we're sweating, and we spend so much time trying to avoid drinking the water we're in that we often neglect to drink regular water once we're out. But it's essential, and having a decent bottle is both a handy reminder and a way of avoiding buying endless disposable ones that could just end up in the sea.

You can use a regular sports bottle, or buy a swimming-specific one that is buoyant in the water, needing to be squeezed or sucked to release the drink. These are great if you're swimming in open water, as they can be chucked from a boat without sinking if they're full.

Tracking devices

You can buy all sorts of swim trackers, from small lap counters that slot onto your index finger and can be tapped with your thumb as you reach the pool end, to high-tech fitness tracking devices that will use GPS to follow your progress across the oceans. Each has its advantages and disadvantages: for example, the TomTom Sports Watch was unfailingly useless at tracking me in the pool, being hopelessly overgenerous with how many lengths I had done and making little sense, yet it proved invaluable when I was swimming in Greece. It had a freestyle mode that simply tracked my route and pace in the sea, showing me afterwards how much I needed to work on my sighting and technique when swimming against currents, as well as letting me know how far I had swum.

There are all sorts of sophisticated watches that will encourage, berate and inform you about every aspect of your swim. They can be useful, but they can also prove a millstone, particularly if you are not training for anything in particular and simply want to enjoy the water. Be warned, too – they often don't track breaststroke, as they need your arm to be exiting the water regularly to pick up the GPS.

CHAPTER FOURTEEN

Leaping In

You think you want to get swimming, or make the move from the pool to the open water, but you don't know where to start. Here are the top ten questions I either had when I was a novice myself, or am now frequently asked, on the subject of where to begin.

1. I want to take part in an event, but do I have to enter a triathlon to do a short organised swim?

No, there are lots of events for swimmers who want to complete shorter distances as part of training for a triathlon. A sprint triathlon swim is 750 metres, a standard is 1.5 kilometres, and an Ironman distance is 3.8 kilometres. Of course – as with my Arun swim experience – this can temper the mood of the event, making for a more competitive atmosphere. There is also the unnerving practice at the start of triathlon events of swimmers swimming *over* each other in their haste to get to the front of the pack. That experience is a big no from me, and I had no qualms about holding back until the alpha crew had set off. Triathletes in training needn't be a reason to put you off taking part in any of these shorter events, though – after all, if you can persuade enough friends to go with you, you have created your own mood.

2. What about if I want to do a longer swim? Or one that is less competitive?

At the other end of the spectrum, the Outdoor Swimming Society and Chill Swim organise longer swims that involve the endurance aspect that triathlon-length swims don't, but with the mood of a festival. The Dart 10K, the Jubilee River Swim (10 kilometres, but doable as a relay), the Bantham Swoosh (6 kilometres) and the Coniston End-to-End (5.25 miles) are as much about the journey as they are about breaking any time limits. Appreciating the natural environment, feeling safe in a long stretch of water that you might not undertake alone, and spending time in the company of other outdoor swimmers – all of these are equal objectives here.

Then there are marathon swims and Channel crossings, which are an altogether bigger undertaking. Channel crossings can be done as a team, or solo. It is a costly and unpredictable business, though – and not one that sounds particularly enjoyable. The course is a busy shipping lane, you can end up swimming for hours longer than you have trained for if the weather is against you, and there is little to see or experience en route. Very few French people care about swimming the Channel, which makes me suspect it's not a goal I would ever like to pursue.

3. I don't care about distances, I just want to swim in amazing places, but safely. How do I get to do that?

A swimming holiday is the route you want to take. SwimTrek is the company that has all but created the market here, but there are others such as the Big Blue (who took me to Greece), Strel Swimming and the US-based SwimVacation who will organise a trip for you. There are also companies such as Swim the Lakes, who arrange shorter day trips for those who want to swim in the Lake District but are anxious about doing it alone.

Most of the international trips will arrange accommodation, boats and guides, as well as having a specific schedule of swims booked with local coastguards for the duration of the trip. To varying degrees they also organise swim coaching, fun afternoons of water sports and special meals out. The UK-based trips often involve nothing but support for the swim, but if it means being able to swim under Durdle Door or along the Thames with safety guides to hand, it is still well worth it.

The idea of going on an adventurous holiday was pretty overwhelming for me, but I spoke at length to J, our guide in Greece, and I have since interviewed Simon Murie, who founded SwimTrek, the company with the greatest experience in this area. Everyone who goes on these trips has the same kind of anxieties: they're worried about being left behind, they're worried about letting the others down, they're worried about swimming in unfamiliar water.

These trips are generally great value for money, though they are still a significant financial outlay. But if you are in a position to go, save up and enjoy!

4. I can't afford a holiday! I just want to get into a lake, river or the sea, but I don't have anyone to go with – is that okay?
It's highly inadvisable to go swimming in open water alone unless you are an exceptionally experienced swimmer in water that you know very well. It's too risky, and also it's quite boring,

not to mention lonely. For the purpose of finding nearby swimmers, the Outdoor Swimming Society is an invaluable resource, and a far more personal touch than Google. Its Facebook group is used not just by new or potential swimmers looking for like-minded souls nearby, but by people all over the country who are going away for a holiday or even on a work trip and want to know if there will be any outdoor swimming going on where they'll be. It is rare that a polite and friendly request goes unanswered, and our informal group in Brighton has welcomed passing swimmers too. Anywhere there is a clean and safe body of water, there will be a swimming group based around it, however informally.

5. How do I know which way the tide is going if I want to get into the sea?
If you already have a swim buddy but just want to get in the water, it is essential to do some research into the local conditions, such as tides and waves. The Magicseaweed app is a wonderful resource for this if you are near the sea rather than rivers, lakes or lidos, and in some instances it even has cameras online so you can actually see the height of the waves you're considering swimming in. Another great website is www.goodbeachguide. co.uk, which lets you know what sort of wildlife you might encounter and also how clean the water is.

If you want to undertake a swim that heads one way and then returns, it is safest (and most enjoyable) to do it so that you have the current helping you on the way back. That way, if the weather changes, or you encounter accident or adventure, you will have natural help getting home. Do note that while the tide is usually taking you one way, a strong wind can override this. In the UK we have two tides a day, and on the south coast where I swim, if the tide is going out, the current is going west. That reverses as the tide comes in. But if it is a particularly windy day, and the wind is blowing from west to east, you may end up getting blown in the opposite direction. The safest thing to do is get in the water, look at the shore, and see which way you float once you have been in for twenty seconds or so. Then head the other way!

Whatever your plans and however far you intend to swim, you should always give a moment's pause to consider what the sea is doing before you get in. Even utterly flat water can have strong currents pulling beneath the surface, and it is unnerving at best, frightening at worst to realise you are swimming home and getting nowhere.

6. What is a rip tide, and how do I deal with one?
Rip tides are basically the consequence of waves hitting the beach entirely parallel to it, and the water beneath the waves then pulling back with exceptional strength and speed. This intense current can pull a swimmer, or someone playing on a lilo in the water, several hundred feet back from the shore in a matter of seconds. If you are a less confident swimmer, deliberately staying where the water is shallow, this is terrifying, and the force of the water means that following your instinct – swimming against the rip towards the shore – is pointless. There is, however, a quick way to get out of the rip: you simply swim to the side, parallel to the beach. Don't even think about trying to get back to the beach until you have swum to the side a good few metres and are no longer in the rip. After that, it should be relatively easy to get back to shore.

Rip tides are sudden and scary, but generally take place on

beaches where the lifeguards know that they are expected and signpost adequately. So don't let them dog your nightmares unduly.

7. What will I want to have with me for when I get out of the water?
If you're swimming in anything but the sunniest of Mediterranean or Caribbean seas, you will probably come out of the water and feel a bit chilly. So the most important things to have with you are a few layers of warm clothing. A couple of sweatshirts will do just as well as a hi-tech fleece if you have space rather than cash to burn. And I prefer putting leggings onto damp legs rather than tracksuit bottoms or jeans, which tend to stick and bunch up while I'm standing on one leg pulling them on. A hat and scarf make a huge difference, as will having a flask of something hot. And Uggs, for so long the dark shame of my wardrobe, are now being used for the purpose they were invented: sliding on for warm toes after sea-bound adventures.

8. Seriously, though, what fish might be in there?
Well, that is half the mystery. And isn't a little mystery half the fun? To speak only of the waters closest to me, an actual dolphin has been spotted several times swimming around the West Pier in Brighton. In UK waters there are very few fish that might actually do you harm, for all that some of them can look pretty ugly (sorry, pike). On the whole, fish will swim away from you before you even spot them – we are so much larger, and considerably scarier, especially in a group.

Occasionally I have a moment of terror that a boisterous seal is about to thump me, but most of the time the thought of seeing fish in the water is part of the excitement. Local lifeguards – or fishermen! – will be able to tell you specifics about where you're swimming, and www.goodbeachguide. co.uk (run in association with the Marine Conservation Society) is a solid starting point for your research.

9. I'm perfectly fine in the pool, thanks, but how do I take things up a notch with my swimming without heading into the wild?
The wisest thing to do is to find your local Masters swimming group. It's like joining a local track club. The group will organise age-categorised training sessions and meets, and will more than keep you on your toes.

10. I have absolutely fallen in love with swimming. What can I read next?
Swimming gets all the best literature. There are novels that have very little to do with swimming but whose authors know the potency of a good splash or a beautiful swimming pool for dramatic effect. The bathing scene in E. M. Forster's *A Room With a View* perfectly encapsulates the temporary delirium of an outdoor swim, and more recently, both Alan Hollinghurst's *The Swimming Pool Library* and Harriet Lane's sinister *Her* make perfect use of the notion of a swimming pool as a sacred space. Below are a few of my favourite swimming-based reads; in addition, any of Oliver Sacks's writing or interviews about swimming are wonderful.

Al Alvarez, *Pondlife: A Swimmer's Journal* (Bloomsbury, 2013)
Alvarez, a distinguished poet and author, describes his regular year-round swims in Hampstead Heath's ponds. It reads as

a diary of his swimming companions and his absolute passion for cold-water swimming, and contains some wonderful meditations on the ageing process and the power of swimming as solace.

Lisa Bier, *Fighting the Current: The Rise of American Women's Swimming* (McFarland, 2011)
Covering a pivotal time for women's swimming, Bier has discovered both wonderful stories and shocking facts. This is a somewhat academic read, but those anecdotes are worth truffling out.

John Cheever, 'The Swimmer' (available on the *New Yorker* archive)
Cheever's iconic short story perfectly captures the idea that if you just go for a really good swim, everything will be okay. Dark and desperate but utterly hypnotic, it is as good a read as it is a terrible training manual.

Lynn Cox, *Grayson* (Harcourt Books)
Writer Sloane Crosley recommended this breathtakingly perfect nugget of a story to me. Lynn Cox, a world-class swimmer, then only a teenager, is taking her morning swim off her local Californian beach when she comes across a baby grey whale, which she names Grayson. It has become separated from its family and starts to follow her. She must keep swimming in order to guide the now tired, hungry and confused Grayson back to its mother. Cox writes exquisitely about the change in the water when she realises the whale is near, as well as doing an exceptional job of calling to

mind the pure exhaustion of a swim of the kind she had that morning.

Roger Deakin, *Waterlog: A Swimmer's Journey Through Britain* (Vintage)
In 1996, nature writer and swimmer Roger Deakin decided to swim the length of Britain – through seas, lakes, tarns, lidos, pools and beyond. It's a social history of a country, a delicious slice of nature writing and a perfect love song to outdoor swimming.

Caitlin Davies, *Downstream: A History and Celebration of Swimming the River Thames* (Aurum Press, 2015)
Another wonderful social history, taking the swimmer's perspective on centuries of life on the River Thames. A friendly tone, some charming anecdotes, and some very thorough research make this as revealing about body ideals, concepts of hygiene, and the class system as it is about what leisure has meant to us over the ages. Davies is also the author of the smaller *Taking the Waters: A Swim Around Hampstead Heath* (Frances Lincoln, 2012), which is specifically about the iconic bathing ponds there.

Diana Nyad, *Find a Way: One Untamed and Courageous Life* (Macmillan, 2016)
It reads like a thriller, but it's all true. Nyad was a world-class swimmer in her twenties, broke the open-ocean world record for both men and women on her thirtieth birthday – and then didn't swim for thirty years. As she hit her sixties, she decided to take on the one challenge that had always eluded her: swimming from Cuba to Florida, without a shark cage.

During the 2016 US presidential campaign, Hillary Clinton cited the book as an inspiration, saying, 'When you're facing big challenges in your life, you can think about Diana Nyad getting attacked by the lethal sting of box jellyfishes, and nearly anything else seems doable in comparison.' She's not wrong.

Leanne Shapton, *Swimming Studies* (Particular Books, 2012)
Shapton's memoir (and art project!) has the same central premise as *Leap In* – learning how to like your body when you're expecting the unfamiliar from it – but from entirely the opposite direction. She was a competitive swimmer as a teenager, nearly making the Olympic team, and then found herself having to relearn how to enjoy swimming without goals as an adult. A combination of her exquisite paintings, photographs of her favourite swimsuits and recollections of important swims, it is a truly beautiful work on swimming.

Lynn Sherr, *Swim: Why We Love the Water* (Public Affairs, 2012)
A potted history and a charming memoir, Sherr's book is sunny-natured and accessible, particularly as it approaches swimming from the perspective of someone who came to the sport late in life. It also has some wonderful illustrations and photographs for the truly nerdy among us.

Charles Sprawson, *Haunts of the Black Masseur* (Vintage, 2000)
A beautiful combination of memoir, history and watery flights of fancy, Sprawson's classic is mesmerising on the bewitching nature of swimming, though it paints an almost exclusively male picture. It's a gorgeous read, but perhaps more

enjoyable if you are already a confident and enthusiastic swimmer.

Jeff Wiltse, *Contested Waters: A Social History of Swimming Pools in America* (University of North Carolina Press, 2010)
The most comprehensive look at the history of public swimming baths in the United States, and the effects of segregation on the nation and its relationship with swimming and pools.

Whatever your tastes, there is a swimming book out there for you to read at the water's edge. But please, don't forget to put it down from time to time, and enjoy the water.

Acknowledgements

This book was written at an unexpectedly sad time, and would never have been finished if not for the endless kindness, silliness and patience of a group of friends for whom I am eternally grateful. Carol Biss, Clare Bennett, Damian Barr, Eleanor Morgan, Euan MacDonald, Eva Wiseman, Georgie Palmer, Helen Chesshire, Jess & Jack Ruston, Jo Rivett, Jojo Moyes, Katie Fraser, Laurence Creamer, Lucy Moses, Melissa Weatherill, Mia Dabrowski, Polly Samson, and Rachel Roberts: thank you, you have no idea how much you helped.

Straddling the divide between friendship and business with extraordinary elegance and warm-heartedness were my editor Jocasta Hamilton and agent Sarah Ballard, whose generosity with both deadlines and solid gold advice most certainly didn't go unnoticed.

Without Patrick, Julia and Kim at Pool to Pier there would be no book, as I would still be unable to swim. Truly, they achieved what seemed impossible, and I am forever in their debt. I have also been lucky enough to find both wisdom and solace in all sorts of fellow swimmers, and these in particular were a huge help during the writing of the book: the team at the Big Blue Swim, the Beyond Wednesdays gang, Celia Smith, Dan Bullock, Rob at the Pells Pool, Simon Murie at Swim Trek, and Vince, Helen and Tess, my Lake District guides!

I would also like to thank the staff at the Agora Clinic in Hove, particularly Mel and Victoria. I will never forget how much kindness you afforded me when I needed it most.

And D, always D.